plant water grow

How Seeds Were Planted and Watered Inside Me... *and God Made Me Grow*

IAN GOLD

Copyright © 2012 by Ian Gold
All Rights Reserved

Published by PlantWaterGrow Publishing.
Attention: Ian Gold 9227 E. Lincoln Ave. Lone Tree, CO, Suite #200, Box #202, Lone Tree, Colorado 80227.

All rights reserved. No part of this book may be reproduced in any form or by any electronic or mechanical means including information storage and retrieval systems without permission in writing from the publisher, except by a reviewer, who may quote brief passages in a review.

ISBN-10: 0983706700 ISBN-13: 9780983706700

Library of Congress Number: 2012902790

Edited by Mike Devries

Unless otherwise noted, all scripture quotations in this publication are taken from the King James Version (kjv). The *Holy Bible, New International Version*® (niv®). Copyright © 1973, 1978, 1984 by International Bible Society. Used by permission of Zondervan. All rights reserved. *New Living Translation* (nlt), copyright © 1971, used by permission of Tyndale House Publishers, Inc., Wheaton, IL 60189, all rights reserved.

I planted the seed, Apollos watered it,

but God made it grow.

1Corinthians 3:6, NIV

TABLE OF CONTENTS

Introduction		1
1	My Journey Begins	5
2	Life Changing Moments	23
3	God Answers Prayer	41
4	A Whole New World	59
5	Deception	73
6	Trip Around The World	87
7	Sex Around the World and Back	107
8	My Surrender	125
9	Chasing Horizons	151
10	The Painful Truth	173
11	Unexpected Encounters	193
12	Through God's Eyes	205
13	Today	229
Immunity		245

INTRODUCTION

No longer employing the full extent of my mental and physical capacity to defend white painted lines on fields full of green grass—as a former Pro Bowl linebacker in the National Football League—*I am now a farmer*. In the fall of 2011, God prompted me to sell my home, along with a majority of my possessions in order to *plant, water, and grow*. You may ask, "Why would anyone choose to walk away from the NFL to become a farmer?!"

The short answer—*a trailer full of faith*.

The long answer—*will be revealed as you read and travel along with me through the first thirty-three years of my life*.

As my last professional football season came to a close in 2007, I thought, *I've spent the last seventeen years of my life leaping, sprinting, sweating, and bleeding on football fields all across the country. Maybe it's time for me to move into the next phase of my journey.* In March 2008, a month after being released by the Denver Broncos, standing at the edge of the rest of my life, I was uncertain whether or not I would ever put on football pads again. *I'm not sure I'll ever play ball again, but one thing is for sure—it feels good to be free!*

For the first time in my life, I had no contractual agreements holding me, bound as with a ball and chain. So finally, with the freedom to come and go without asking for permission from coaches and athletic trainers, I took a firm hold of my destiny!

With freedom beckoning, and after spending a few weeks contemplating my future, I arrived at a crossroad. *I have two choices: I can leap forward and move on with the rest of my life; or I can continue making money, since there are still teams interested in hiring me to play ball for them.* Prayerfully considering both options, the thought of walking away from football—the one constant in my life—led me to this question: *If I did choose to retire, what's next?*

During the weeks and months that followed, I often slept with eyes wide open; daydreaming and brainstorming of ways I could help people. I thought about the challenges I faced as a child, thinking of ways I could help kids and teens realize their dreams of attending college, despite the socio-economic constraints. I thought of ways to blanket orphans and widows with unconditional love and support, and even ways to jumpstart our country's choking economy by utilizing cause-related ideas and concepts.

"WAIT a minute! I have a brain!" I exclaimed. "I can't believe it's been nearly eight years since I've used my intellect to think about anything besides football."

While mulling over ideas of how to help people, I instinctively began reflecting on the direction and experiences of the first twenty-nine years of my life. My time of reflection produced three extremely important questions:

1. *What have I done with my life up to this point?*
2. *What type of man have I become?*
3. *Where am I headed?*

With a shovel in hand, the answers to these questions would soon be unearthed. When I think of the winding road I traveled to arrive at this point of my life's journey, I am reminded of a man named Saul of Tarsus, also known as Paul. One day, while Saul was traveling on the road to Damascus, he encountered Jesus Christ—and his life was forever changed. After committing many horrible acts of sin—actions in direct opposition to God's laws and commandments—Saul said,

> *This is a faithful saying and worthy of all acceptation, that Christ Jesus came into the world to save sinners; of whom I am chief (1 Timothy 1:15).*

If Saul is the chief of sinners, then because of the many senseless acts of sin I have committed in my short lifetime—I am the lieutenant. Guilty of using an abundance of time, zeal, resources, and influence for selfish purpose and gain, there too came a day in my journey when I had an encounter with Christ.

As I pour out my heart onto these pages, there are two things I must convey about the journey I am about to share with you:

1. *I DO NOT blame anyone other than myself for the suffering and pain I have caused others and myself, nor the negative circumstances that have come as a result of my foolish actions.*

2. *I am in no way celebrating the poor judgments I have made up until this point in my life, nor the senseless actions I have committed as a result of my numerous selfish decisions.*

What have I done with my life up until this point? What type of person have I become? Where am I headed? These are questions that ultimately led me to discover my immunity—and the *unrelenting, unfailing, undying, unconditional, and everlasting love of God.*

And with that, let the journey begin.

CHAPTER 1
MY JOURNEY BEGINS

On August 23, 1978, I was born in Ann Arbor, MI to a young couple that had been married in "wholly dysfunctional matrimony" for just over a year. My mother, who gave me my name, held me gently in her secure arms until I could crawl, walk, talk, and think for myself. Many of the memories from my early childhood have faded over the years, one, however, stands clear. By the time I reached five-years-old, I distinctly remember wondering—*Why are mom and dad always yelling and fighting?* Most of my memories from the earliest periods of my life's journey are extremely painful. Many involved my dad and his excessive abuse of alcohol. His abuse, however, extended far beyond alcohol—as he also physically and verbally abused my mother.

My dad was not around much. One of the few times he decided to come home, I remember him sending my brothers—Jason and Jeremy, twins a year older than me, and Cory, a year younger than me—and myself to our bedroom. I can still feel the intensity in his voice as he stood in the doorway.

"Don't come out of this room, or I'm gonna tear y'all tails up!' he warned. Shortly after our bedroom door closed, *it* began.

"I'm gonna call the police!" my mother screamed.

"So what! Call 'em!" my dad shouted.

While the yelling and fighting continued, I remember sitting on the edge of my bed. There I sat, close to the bedroom door, listening to my mother's screams and desperate cries for help as she attempted to defend herself from her husband's abuse. Filled with anger and rage, one isolated thought pulsed repeatedly through my mind. *I wish I were bigger. I wish I were bigger. I wish I WERE BIGGER!* Wanting to do something—anything—to prevent the abuse my mother undeservingly suffered, but fearing what our dad would do to us, we sat helplessly in our bedroom, silently waiting for the screaming to cease. Continually listening to my mother's cries for help, painful seeds of violence and anger were planted inside me.

As I write this, remembering the details from the last time my parents fought, I can still feel the chills I felt one day while sitting in the back seat of my grandmother's car with my brothers. Looking out of the back window, I saw a car skid around the corner of the parking lot—the driver was my mother's youngest brother. He got out of the car, with what looked like a wrench or crowbar in his hand. He approached my dad, and then the two of them disappeared from sight. After getting out of grandma's car, once it was safe, I walked past my dad's broken glasses on the black asphalt, I wondered, *How did dad's glasses end up broken on the ground?*

Once inside our apartment, my brothers and I sat on the pink colored couch in our living room. A tall man dressed in a dark blue uniform then asked each of us the same question, "Who do you want to live with, young man?" Once it came to my turn, he looked me in the eye.

"Who do you want to live with?"

"My dad," I said.

Shocked by my response, everyone in the room immediately looked at me as if I had given the officer the wrong answer. I quickly corrected myself.

"No wait, I want to live with mom!"

Having just turned five years old, I had no clue as to why I had to answer such a perplexing question. In spite of the police being called to our small apartment on several different occasions due to my dad's violent temper and abusive nature, I still loved my dad very much. I would have given up every last one of my toys just to be able to sit and watch Westerns with him. Spending time with my dad, however, turned out to be a childhood dream that never came true.

After six long, horrifying, painful years, my mother found the courage and strength to walk away from her extremely troubled, dysfunctional marriage. She was a strong woman, unwilling to live in fear any longer! Unbeknownst to me at the time, her courageous decision would be the first of several pivotal turning points in my life's journey. From this point, until my final year of middle school, we moved back and forth between Ann Arbor and Ypsilanti, Michigan.

My relationship with my older brothers only added to the pain of my early childhood. As twins, they were inseparable. They slept in the same room together, played together, and even shared all of the same friends. Whenever they would go outside to play, they would attempt to leave me at home with Cory. Sadly, I was too consumed with my own emotions to stop and think about my youngest brother's feelings, as he was often left home alone. "Why can't I go with you guys?" I would often ask, receiving no response. Unfortunately, they never wanted much to do with me. As a result, painful seeds of rejection and loneliness were planted inside me.

I never felt more rejected than I did one day in the middle of the heat of summer. I was twelve-years-old and we were visiting my grandparents' house on Hill Street in Ypsilanti. My brothers, cousins, and I loved playing basketball. On this particular day, my older brother Jeremy, my cousin, and I made the short walk up "the hill"—a steep asphalt street—to play a game of basketball with other kids from around the neighborhood. At one point during the game, my cousin and I got into a shoving match. Standing face-to-face and chest-to-chest against one another, appearing as though we were going to fight, Jeremy ran over and nudged my cousin out of the way. Then he got up in *my* face and shouted, "Ian you better leave him alone! If you wanna fight him, you gotta fight me first!"

Hearing those words made my already fragile heart feel as if it had been ripped out of my chest and slammed onto the sizzling hot asphalt. *No one has ever stood up for me, and now my very own brother stands up for my cousin instead of me?* Embarrassed and heartbroken, I quickly turned and walked back down the steep asphalt hill to my grandparents' house, fighting back tears the entire way. *How could my own brother treat me like that?* I wondered.

Opening the screen door to my grandparent's front porch, I made sure I was alone and the tears began streaming down my face. A seed of humiliation was planted inside me—as I had never felt more humiliated, or more unloved, in my life. *Why does he hate ME so much?* I screamed silently. *I wonder if he doesn't want me to be his brother anymore.* Bawling my eyes out on my grandparents' front porch, feeling confused, enraged, and heart-broken, I thought, *Nobody likes me. My own brother doesn't even care about me. Why am I even alive?*

When my mother arrived, I carefully stuffed my heart back into its place. Attempting to hide all evidence of heartache and pain, I did my best to hide the scar left from the seed of humiliation that had just been planted within me. This routine of suppressing and hiding my emotions became the way I dealt with pain.

While Jeremy's words and actions ripped my heart out of my chest and slammed it to the asphalt, it was the oldest of the twins, Jason, who finally finished it off. Everybody loved

Jason. He had all the good looks, the respect of his friends, and tons of athletic talent. I would have given up my most prized possession, my very first trumpet—which my mother purchased for me at a garage sale—just to feel loved, respected, or even liked by my oldest brother.

There were times I would follow him and his friends to the park. I would always walk about twenty yards behind—close enough to catch up with him if he tried to lose me, but far enough away to run if he tried to chase me down and beat me up for following him. I followed him to the baseball fields in the spring. I followed him to the neighborhood swimming pool in the summer. I followed him to the best sledding hills in the winter. I would have followed him off the edge of a cliff just to get him to be my friend.

No matter how Jason treated me, I always tried my very best to earn his love and respect. Once, with hopes of impressing him so he would select me to play on his basketball team, I spent an entire summer dribbling around our neighborhood alone. I must have dribbled that basketball up and down every sidewalk in the neighborhood. Despite all of my efforts, he never wanted me on his team. His utter disdain for me eventually became noticeable to all of our cousins, teammates, and even to friends from school. *Is there something wrong with me?* I wondered.

Seeds of fear, shame and embarrassment were planted inside me, as I became embarrassed, ashamed, and even afraid to be myself. I became extremely self-conscious of the way I smelled, looked, walked, and talked. If I could have changed whatever he didn't like about me, I would have in a heartbeat. I found myself walking around on eggshells all of the time—*I hope he doesn't tell anybody I peed in the bed last night. Please don't let him talk about my big nose today.*

Whenever I would see my brother laughing with our cousins or a group of his friends, I always assumed they were laughing at me. Paranoid, insecure, and fearful of being ridiculed, I found myself with very little or no self-confidence. I eventually developed a noticeable stutter in my speech. Living in constant fear of being ridiculed for stuttering, I kept my comments and answers short. I even reached a point where I wouldn't dare to speak without silently rehearsing my comments or answers before speaking them aloud, to ensure I would speak articulately.

Regardless of how traumatic my relationship with my older brothers was during my childhood, my mother did her best to "train us up in the way we should go". Named after her mother, Celia Mae, my mom planted seeds of faith within the four of us just as her late mother and father did with their twelve children. My grandmother, "Mother Frye," was a retired housemaid and a spiritual mother to many; and my grandfather, affectionately known as "Papa," was an elder in the church. Whether my brothers and I wanted to or not, we were in service every Sunday—and even some Saturdays. We participated in every Christmas and Easter program and we sang in the choir. My mother would make us practice our singing constantly, whether at home or riding in our car. I felt like we were being groomed to become the next boy band. On several occasions, my brothers and I were called to sing a selection in front of the entire congregation.

"At this time," the announcer would say, making my stomach twist into a knot, "we're going to have a selection from the Gold brothers!" Making our way up to the platform, we'd sing our hearts out as our mother beamed with pride.

While sitting in Sunday morning service, my brothers, cousins and I were naturally bored—we didn't understand much about God or preaching. To keep from falling asleep, we kept ourselves entertained with games like hangman, tic-tac-toe, and thump. What we *really* wanted was to be outside wrestling, getting grass stains all over our dress clothes, racing barefoot down the middle of the neighborhood streets, or challenging each other to climb up on top of my great-grandmother's roof.

My great-grandmother earned the nickname "Granny Sees" because she could see us misbehaving even in her sleep! Whenever Granny heard footsteps on top of her roof or the sound of branches breaking, she would stand behind her dusty screened door and shout, "Get outta' my tree!" or "Get down off of that roof! I'm goin' to tell 'L' (Granny's nickname for my grandfather)!" And whenever Granny told Papa, we all knew somebody—or everybody—would receive a serious spanking.

Keeping us in Sunday service for two or even three hours was like trying to put a pig on a diet—which would only happen if the pig were forced. But during those Sunday services, even though I struggled to pay attention, I did manage to learn a few helpful ways to cope with my feelings of loneliness, rejection and anger.

One humid Sunday afternoon, our entire family attended a service in Muskegon, Michigan, approximately three hours northwest of Ann Arbor. That morning I learned one of the more powerful lessons in my life—the power of "hugging myself."

Upon arriving and entering the sanctuary, my brothers and I rushed to take a seat on one of the old squeaky, hardwood benches. With no air conditioning to speak of in the church, several people waved fans back and forth in an effort to cool themselves from the sweltering heat. When the offering period came to an end, the pastor introduced the guest speaker. Standing before the entire congregation in his long white robe, the speaker said, "There were four little boys who just walked by the offering table. I believe they are all brothers."

"Yeeesss," my grandmother responded aloud while looking back at my mother.

"One of you," he continued, "is always getting into trouble at school and at home. You feel as if you are all alone and you really miss your dad. Now, whichever one of you I'm talking about, I want you to come on up here to the altar."

Everyone in my family immediately turned and fixed their eyes on me. As they each glared at me, the tiny seeds of fear, shame and embarrassment within me, began to take root, causing me to melt in my pew. *I'm not going up there!*

The guest pastor patiently waited and the organist played softly, but I ignored his request—even though I could feel my mother's eyes piercing me like a goad. Then my mother, leaning over to me, whispered to me in her all-too-familiar "I'm not gon' tell you again" tone:

"Ian, get up there. Now!"

I took a deep breath, stepped out into the aisle, and walked at a snail's pace toward the front of the small building.

While it had taken me only a few seconds to reach the front of the sanctuary during the offering period, this second trip to the front seemed to last an eternity. When I finally arrived at the front, standing nervously with my hands clutched together and my head held low, the pastor began to speak:

> *The Lord sees your heart and he knows all of the hurt and pain you feel. He told me to tell you this: Whenever you feel like you are all alone and no one is there for you and whenever you miss your dad, all you have to do is hug yourself. Jesus wants you to know that He is always there for you and whenever you hug yourself, you are hugging Him!*

Then he asked me to hug myself. As I stood at the altar with my back facing the congregation, a tiny seed of *God's love* was planted inside me, as I wrapped my arms around myself. Tears began to trickle down my face. Out of desperation to be unconditionally loved and accepted, I received and immediately believed his words with *all* of my heart—and a seed of belief was planted within me. From that day forward, whenever I found myself feeling the pain of rejection from my older brothers or the mixed feelings of anger and sadness generated by my dad's absence, I would pause and wrap my arms around myself for comfort. I'd embrace myself for a while, the tears would pour out, and then I always felt better. Even as I type these words—with tears sliding down my face—I embrace myself. *Lord, thank you for all of the times you've held me when I needed you most.*

Despite the fact that hugging myself helped to calm and console me at times, roots from seeds of anger, rejection, and loneliness, began digging their way deep inside me, which resulted in me getting into trouble at school. As the result of my misbehavior in grade school, my mother spent countless hours spanking me and having heart-to-heart talks with me—all in an effort to get me to start behaving properly. In fact, one Sunday evening my mother asked the entire congregation to pray for me:

"I give honor to God, the pastor, and the saints. Please pray for my children and me. One of my sons is having a really difficult time in school and at home. I talk to him and I beat him. I talk to him and I beat him. I just don't know what else to do besides pray and ask the Lord for help! So I am asking for you all to please pray for him and pray for my strength in the Lord."

Turning, the entire congregation immediately looked back at the four of us. And when my three brothers turned and looked at me, I sank down into the pew, signaling to everyone I was the one about whom my mother was referring. As I sat there feeling horrible, I thought, *Wow, I made mom cry in front of all of these people. I gotta stop gettin' in trouble!*

In addition to wanting love and affection, I wanted to be heard. There were a ton of unanswered questions bouncing around inside of my mind and heart—*Why did mom and dad get divorced? Why did dad hit mom? Why don't Jason and Jeremy like me? Why do I have a half-sister who's not my mom's daughter?* But sadly, nobody took the time to listen to me—my parents remained divorced and my older brothers continued rejecting me.

Uncertain whether my questions were safe to ask, or even to whom I could turn for answers, I decided to keep them buried deep inside, close to my damaged heart. I eventually did manage to figure out the answer to one of my questions. During a car ride when I was ten years old, I wondered, *How could I have a sister six months younger than me, but eleven months older than my youngest brother?* Instead of asking my parents, I decided to practice my math skills. Calculating the months using my fingers and adding the fact that my sister and I did not have the same mother but did have the same dad, my eyes widened. *Wait a minute! So that means dad had a baby with another woman while he was still married to mom! Then he came back and had Cory with mom!*

As this stunning revelation set in, a seed of sadness was planted inside me—as I felt sad for my mother. Not only was my dad physically and verbally abusive, he also scarred her emotionally by committing adultery. Sadly, my mother wasn't the only person my dad left emotionally scarred. As the years progressed, there came a point in which my dad's empty promises to my brothers and me left me feeling unloved, unwanted, and unimportant to him. He broke promise after promise to us.

"Yes, son, your father's gonna pick you up this weekend."

"Yes, son, your father's gonna come to your game Friday night."

With my bag packed, at times, I waited in vain for his arrival. Finally, I gave up and as I unpacked my clothes and placed them back in my dresser, seeds of doubt and distrust were planted within me—causing my heart to grow cold toward my dad.

Contrarily, many seeds of joy and laughter were planted inside me during my childhood. One of my fondest memories from childhood involved Papa—may he rest in peace. One summer day my mother dropped my brothers and me off at the neighborhood recreation center, as she often did. We would spend entire summer days there playing with our cousins and other kids from different areas of the city. After a couple of hours of being at the center on this particular day, my cousins, brothers, and I decided we wanted to go to our grandparent's house, which was definitely *not* within walking distance. One of my cousins called my grandparents house to see if someone would come and pick up the group of us. Papa answered the phone.

"Okay, I'll be there *reckly* [shortly]," he said.

When he arrived at the recreation center, all of us piled into his car and Papa began driving back to Hill Street. Suddenly, he developed an urgent need to use the restroom. Out of desperation, he pulled into a nearby gas station.

"Papa," said one of the voices from the back of the car, "looks like it's closed."

Instead of driving to another gas station, Papa reached underneath his seat and grabbed something. As he sat there quietly, I glanced over to see what Papa had in his hand, and what exactly he was doing. When I saw him going to the bathroom in a bag, I turned toward the passenger side window and let out a small chuckle, which caused a chain reaction with everyone else in the car. Unsuccessfully attempting to keep our laughter silent to ourselves, Papa became incensed.

"What ya' nasty selves laughin' at?" he shouted. "Ya'll betta' hope ya'll don't have to use a bag one day!"

Another fond memory from my childhood involved going over to my grandparents' house every Sunday after service—here is where I gained an appreciation for family and good ol' southern cookin'. Visits to Grandma's always eased the agony of sitting through a three-hour service because I knew that once I got to Grandma's house, I would get to play with my cousins and eat all of my favorite foods. Every Sunday my grandmother would prepare a meal similar to a Thanksgiving Day feast—for at least twenty people. She cooked and cooked throughout the night for us—turkey, pot roast, ham, smothered pork chops, fried chicken, greens, sweet potatoes, fried corn, sweet potato pies and peach cobbler—you name it, Grandma cooked it! After one of my aunts would summon everyone into the dining room, Papa would then bless the food and—being the generous man that he was—often say, "Eat all ya' wont." And if somebody came strolling in late, unless they called ahead of time and asked someone to save them a plate of food, there was no food left. There was no such thing as leftovers at Grandma and Papa's house!

Speaking of food, to most people it's still a mystery how my mother kept food on the table and clothes on the four of us. For my brothers and me, however, there is no mystery at all—her faith in Christ and a whole lot of prayer kept us fed and clothed. There were times when my brothers and I would come home from school only to realize we had no electricity or running water in our apartment. Being the problem solvers we were, we immediately got on the phone, called our mother at work and explained the emergency. As always, she responded in the same casual tone, "Oh okay. I'll take care of it." Sure enough, by the time my mother got home, the water or electricity would magically work again. *Wow!* I thought. *How does mom do that?*

Of course, my brothers and I always had our own ideas about how the problem had been caused and ultimately repaired.

"Somethin' was probably wrong with the plumbing in the entire building and maintenance must've fixed it," one of us would guess.

"The power must have been out in the whole neighborhood and Mom got the electric company to come out and fix it," another would suggest.

None of us had any idea that she barely made enough money to keep the lights on, feed us, and keep clothes on our backs. My mother often brought home brown boxes of cheese and white boxes of powdered milk, which I later learned she received from the government welfare system. I also recall countless days and nights hearing my mother on the phone—talking and listening—in an effort to give and receive encouragement. I never stuck around long enough to listen because she sometimes went on for well over an hour. While I may not have truly understood what it meant to edify and encourage others at the time, seeds of edification and encouragement were planted inside me.

Often times, when I heard my mother on the phone, I knew that it wouldn't be long before she began to fervently pray and cry out to the Lord with whomever was on the other end of the line. *I don't know what praying does, but it must be helping mom because she sure prays a lot,* I thought.

While witnessing my mother praying to God as a little boy, a seed of prayer was planted deep inside me. And as I grew older, the seed of prayer blossomed within me. Whenever I found myself alone in my room, usually because of my misbehavior, I would pray, *God, please allow mom and dad to get back together again.* Or, *Lord, please send me a best friend.* Or *God, I don't know if you can really hear me, but I am just doing what I see my mother do. So please answer my prayer.* Even though I could not quite pray like my mother, I desperately believed God would one day hear and answer my prayers.

Unbeknownst to me at the time, my dad being absent for the majority of my childhood and adolescent years, and my older brothers not wanting much to do with me, compelled me to seek for love from a man I could not see with my eyes, named Jesus Christ.

CHAPTER 2
LIFE CHANGING MOMENTS

Moving is an overwhelming task—even if you only move once or twice in a lifetime. In my case, however, we moved around quite a bit when I was a child. At the time, I wasn't really sure why we moved so much, but I later learned that it had a lot to do with safety, rent prices, and apartment size—as well as roach and bug problems. Yet, no matter how many times we moved, my mother always paid special attention to the quality of education provided by the school districts. The greatest move we ever made came just months before my tenth birthday. Living in Ypsilanti at the time, my mother gathered my brothers and me together for a family meeting to ask us a question.

"What would you guys think about me going to school at the University of Michigan?"

Being a huge Michigan Wolverine fan, I immediately began leaping and jumping around the living room of our apartment with joy. *GO BLUE!* I might have even sung a portion of "The Victors," Michigan's fight song—as the seed of joy within me received water. I absolutely loved the Wolverines!

Shortly after my outburst, she asked, "What do you guys think about moving to Ann Arbor?" Again, I exploded with excitement! This time I leaped with even greater joy because my dad, who at the time was working on his Master's degree at the University of Michigan, lived in Ann Arbor! *Now I'll be able to see dad more!* So, with that, we made the move to 1920 McIntyre Dr. in the University of Michigan's north campus family housing development. My mother began her classes, while my brothers and I enrolled into Logan Elementary School. I got to see my dad every other weekend. Finally, all was well.

Or so I thought…

The every other weekend visits with my dad only lasted a year or so. And my behavioral issues, instead of getting better, seemed to worsen. I got into trouble for a number of petty reasons. A kid would call my mother a name and I would start a fight. My teachers would give me instructions and I would talk back. Roots from the seeds of violence and anger, which were planted by witnessing domestic violence as a young child, began to dig deeper. Due to my misbehavior and negative attitude, I ended up spending a great deal of time in the principal's office and in-school suspension. As a result, my teachers repeatedly summoned my mother to "personalized" parent-teacher conferences. My aggression toward other students and my disruptive behavior quickly became the topic of everyday conversation around our house. So my mother continued the cycle of talking to me and beating my behind. Mama didn't play! Raising four boys by herself, her mindset was simple, "Better I beat ya'll's behinds so the police won't have to one day!"

It didn't help, though. My behavior turned into a vicious cycle which lasted for five-years. The cycle went like this: I would get into trouble at school, I would come home, and my mother would talk to me about whatever I had done wrong during the school day, and then she would tear my tail up! Then she would have the audacity to come into my room five or ten minutes later and say, "Now, I want you to know how much it really hurts me to have to beat your behin'." *Huh? Then let me whoop your behin' and then we'll see if it hurts the same!*

There's a saying: "It takes a village to raise a child." In my case it was definitely true. There were many people who were instrumental in assisting my mother's efforts to help change my behavior. One of the first people who confronted me about my misbehavior was my sixth grade homeroom teacher at Clague Middle School, Mr. Raymond Pipkin. One day after hearing about my constant misbehaving, he asked to speak to me out in the hallway. As I walked out into the empty hallway and stood up against a white cement wall, he grabbed the front of my shirt. Putting his finger into my face, he tore into me:

Do you know how much hurt and pain you're causing your mother by getting into trouble? Do you realize how difficult your mother already has it raising four boys alone and going to U of M as a single, black mother? I'd better not hear about you getting into any more trouble! Do you hear me? I expect more from you! You should want to make your mother proud and help make her life easier!

Despite hearing similar remarks from other individuals, this encounter served as the first time a strong, educated, black man—other than my dad—had been firm with me. God used those five minutes in the hallway with Mr. Pipkin, as a catalyst for a much-needed detour from the path down which I was headed. Shortly after receiving love, albeit tough love, from Mr. Pipkin, the moment came in which I decided to permanently change my behavior.

After climbing into my top bunk one night, each of us exchanged our shouts of goodnight, which would often take up to five minutes or more:

"Goodnight, Mom!"

"Goodnight, Jeremy!"

"Goodnight, Jason!"

"Goodnight, Cory!"

"Goodnight, Ian!"

After falling fast asleep on this particular night, I woke up to the familiar clicking sound of my mother's typewriter—*tap...tap...tappity...tap.* As the dim light found its way from my mother's bedroom, down the short hallway, and passed the doorway to my bedroom, for the first time ever, I laid there buried beneath my covers, thinking, *Wow, Mom is typing a paper in the middle of the night! I wonder if she ever goes to sleep?* My mother was not a very fast typist, as she later told me that it would often take her several hours to type a single page—so I guess it's fair to say she didn't get much sleep. Under my covers, my thoughts continued, *Wait a minute. Mom wakes us up in the morning, gets us off to school, then she goes to class—only to come home to deal with negative reports from my teachers at school. All this, not to mention she cooks dinner, makes sure we all do our homework and chores. Then she only gets four or five hours of sleep before she has to wake up—in the middle of the night—to do her own homework.*

Submersed in my thoughts, my mother became my hero.

I finally began to realize the extent to which my misbehavior had been negatively affecting my mother, and a seed of compassion was planted inside me. I decided to try my hardest to stay out of trouble. A lot of people were counting on me to change my behavior—my mother and my sixth grade homeroom teacher, not to mention an entire congregation of people whom my mother had enlisted to pray for me.

Even though I constantly found myself in trouble throughout middle school, I still managed to have fun with my buddies. I will never forget all of the laughs, especially during first period lunch. Whether we were beat-boxing and drumming on the cafeteria tables or racing to see who could drink their carton of milk the fastest, we always kept one another amused. I even created dance routines with my friends, which we perfected and performed during middle school dances to impress the girls. Yet with all of this, perhaps the highlight of it all was my first kiss.

Like most boys, middle school was when my desire to chase girls began to emerge. While I knew nothing about sex, I became determined to find a girl who was willing to have some form of intimate encounter with me. At the age of twelve, after hearing rumors about a certain girl who had a reputation for hooking up with guys, I made it a point to get her attention. After we expressed a mutual interest in spending some time together, the next day my hormones and I came up with a plan—I would purposely miss the school bus after school let out. This way, I could walk her home.

As we walked together in total silence—there's not much to talk about when you're twelve years old—I began to panic and thought: *What in the world am I doing? What if her parents come home? I know what I'll do—I'll just kiss her and tell her I have to go home.* As we got closer and closer to her place, after intentionally stalling in the parking lot of her apartment complex, it happened. We kissed! Pondering the moment, I thought, *Wow, my first kiss—standing outside in the cold, freezing my butt off, and with a girl's tongue in my mouth. Her braces felt weird!*

Distracted by my moment of excitement, I failed to notice the small seed of lust that had been planted deep within me in that moment. Nevertheless, after finally kissing a girl, I became a hero to myself—the champion of my own heart.

One noticeable reward of my first kiss was the validation from my buddies. After sharing the news, I immediately became a member of the cool crowd at school—the kids who gave themselves the right to label and categorize all other students. Sad to say, my middle school had a few different labels and categories for students: the cool kids, the troublemakers, and the rejects. Having been one of the best athletes in school caused most kids to think, "Ian's in the cool crowd." But the harsh reality was, in spite of what my peers believed, *I was a self-proclaimed reject*. My older brothers wanted nothing to do with me, I didn't have a girlfriend, and we were poor. At the time, I had absolutely no self-confidence.

Eventually, my self-perception as a reject motivated me to get involved with some of the troublemakers. I became a bully. I acted out—cursing, picking fights with smaller and weaker kids, tripping kids in the hallway, and even pulling someone's chair away from them as they sat down. Was I really a "reject"? Should I have allowed my socio-economic status to make me think less of myself? Certainly not. In the end, however, I made the mistake of allowing the ideas of my peers, society, and even my own brothers affect how I felt and what I believed about myself.

I mistreated other kids, to make them feel the same rejection and loneliness I felt. Being mean to other students allowed me to gain the attention and respect I craved from my peers. Of course, it turned out to be the wrong type of attention and notoriety. Feeling bad about bullying other kids—and realizing that they didn't deserve to be mistreated anymore than I did—I decided to find more constructive ways to release my negative energy and frustrations—and I found it in sports.

Following my seventh grade year, my mother graduated from the University of Michigan and found a job teaching English at a middle school in northern Virginia. By this time, despite having crushes on a few different girls, I hadn't kissed anyone else. But what I did become more and more aware of was my strong athletic ability. Having only played basketball throughout elementary and middle school, shortly after getting acclimated to my new surroundings and making new friends, one of my buddies asked, "Dude, have you ever played football?"

"Nope," I replied. "We didn't have football at my middle school in Michigan."

"Well, you can hit people as hard as you want and not get into trouble," he responded.

All of the pent up, explosive anger toward my dad which I had bottled up and the feelings of rejection and loneliness from the way my older brothers treated me came to surface.

"Where do I sign up?!"

So at the age of thirteen, a seed of brutality was planted inside me, as I put on my first set of football pads with absolutely no idea how far my ability to sprint, hit, and think quickly on my feet would carry me.

Around the same time I began playing football, I also began making occasional trips to the mall with my older brothers and cousins—as my cousin's mother, my mother's older sister, decided to move to Virginia along with us. Each of us would comment to the others, "I'm gonna get the most phone numbers today because I'm a 'mac daddy' and girls love me the most!" But our competition was not limited to malls. It took place everywhere we went—department stores, picnics, school dances, you name it. We even tried to get telephone numbers during Sunday morning services. Wherever there were girls, the game was on. As I entered high school, getting phone numbers from girls eventually developed in me a *false* sense of confidence and validation, which became a catalyst for my growing desire to chase girls.

As is the case with many young adolescent boys, up to this point in my life my mind had become consumed with fantasies. I often hoped and dreamed of becoming like one of the many fictitious super heroes I watched in various cartoons and movies. But, after learning that spinach would never give me super strength—and that green rocks would never make me weak—there were not many truths left for me to hold on to upon completing middle school.

Just before my freshman year in high school, fed up with the cost of living in Virginia, my mother accepted a teaching position at a middle school back in Michigan. Following the move back home, we moved in with my grandparents on Hill Street until my mother could find a place for us to live. Shortly after getting all of our furniture stored in my grandparents' garage, and with the school year about to begin, my mother quickly enrolled my older brothers and I into the same school she attended as a teenager—Ypsilanti High School. We only attended Ypsi for a few months, however, as my mother found an apartment in Belleville, a small, neighboring town with only one high school. We moved to Belleville at the end of my first semester and my mother enrolled us into Belleville High School. Little did I know, moving to Belleville would become another key turning point in my life's journey.

When I first walked into Belleville High, I saw photos of tigers all around the school. And having a love for lions, I thought, *Tigers are close enough*. Excited to become a Tiger, I tried out for the basketball team since football season had just come to an end. I made the basketball team and donned the black and orange for the first time, easily making new friends. Much like myself, most of my new teammates were extremely competitive and most participated in more than one sport. In addition to our love for sports, my teammates and I also shared a love for girls.

In high school, the "girl game" had become even more serious. In order to be considered one of the guys, I now needed to convince a girl to do a whole lot more than kiss. Being content with kissing girls, however, and absolutely terrified by the thought of attempting anything more, I decided not to play the game. *I'm not a mac daddy—I'm only a freshman. Besides, there's going to be plenty of time for me to chase girls one day.* This statement was a premonition of what awaited me in the years to come.

Almost everybody in the school knew me as "the twins' little brother who runs real fast and stutters when he speaks." The truth is my stutter had become so bad that it began to affect most of my attempts to communicate. Once, during a speech I delivered to a group of elementary school students on behalf of a drug awareness organization, I began to have trouble getting a word out. When I finally did, the small gym filled with students sitting on the floor erupted with high-pitched laughter. Hearing the children mimic and make fun of me watered the seeds of shame and embarrassment within me. There I stood, frozen in total humiliation. *Can someone else please finish speaking?* I thought. Unfortunately, the teachers and administrators eventually quieted the kids to give me the opportunity to finish.

As time progressed, I found that although stuttering in front of a group of elementary school kids was embarrassing, I could handle it. On the other hand, the embarrassment that came when I talked to my friends and teammates about girls was absolute torture. Because of my decision to remain a virgin, I did my best to avoid conversations with the guys at school who talked of all their different encounters because they would usually end up making fun of my virginity. They talked about going over to their girlfriends' house when her parents went out of town for the weekend. They talked about the girls they made out with behind the bleachers. They talked about the girls they experimented with in the backseats of their cars. So instead of gossiping about girls, I decided to focus all my time and energy on sports—and what was left of my time and energy on my grades.

When it came to sports, all of the anger pinned deep inside of me—thoughts of my dad abusing my mother when I was a child—exploded in every way imaginable on the field. Whenever I thought of sitting on the edge of my bed, listening to my mother screaming for help, I sprinted faster, jumped higher, and hit harder to defeat any opponent who stood in my way. Practicing against my brothers, Jason and Jeremy planted seeds of competitiveness and vengefulness within me. Anytime I had an opportunity to face one of them during football or basketball practice, I tried to physically punish them for all of the years they made me feel inadequate, rejected, and alone. In fact, the competition between my twin brothers was one of the secrets to my success on the football field and track. Whenever I thought of the pain and hurt my brothers caused me as a child, no opponent could keep me from crossing the finish line first or from getting into the end zone.

Although I never played baseball, rounding the bases with a girl became more and more tempting. Regardless of my efforts to avoid the issue of sex in conversation, I could not escape thinking about it. Everywhere I looked—television, school, the locker room—thoughts and images of sex found their way inside my head.

I remember visiting my friend's house one day and as he talked about sex in front of his father, I sat quietly and blushed as I listened to him. Then, much to my surprise, he said, "Oh, Dad! I almost forgot to tell you—Ian is a virgin!"

As my friend laughed uncontrollably, I lowered my head as his laughter watered the seeds of embarrassment and humiliation rooted deep within me. I responded, "So what! There's nothing wrong with me waiting 'til I'm married!"

My buddy disregarded my comment and continued laughing hysterically. But to my surprise, my friend's father said, "I'm proud of you, Ian! Make sure you stay that way too, because there's nothing wrong with being a virgin." I appreciated his words of encouragement, but I could not get the sound of my friend's laughter out of my head. Sadly, it didn't stop there. Whether in the locker room, on the practice field, or on a bus ride to a game, I became the brunt of jokes. It seemed as if the entire world knew I was a virgin. I was an easy target and that made high school pretty tough for me.

Due to constantly being made fun of, coupled with my growing curiosity as to why everybody always talked about sex, one night during my junior year I decided to try masturbating for the first time. It felt so good that my appetite to try the real thing increased—thus, watering the seed of lust within me. As a result, I began having regular make-out sessions with a girl who gave me rides home after school. I wasn't exactly interested in dating her. In fact, I didn't even understand the point of dating. As time passed, I continued to become more and more intimate with girls who were willing, getting closer to having intercourse with each subsequent girl.

Up until this point, the greatest challenge of my life had been trying to overcome the hurt, pain, rejection, and loneliness caused by the events of my childhood. Now, dealing with my sexuality was my greatest challenge. One day I reached a breaking point. While walking off of the football field after practice, one of my teammates started making fun of me. Typically, I would have walked away. But, having reached my limit with all of the jokes and taunting, I started making fun of him in return. It felt good to stand up for myself for once. But this particular teammate was about twice my weight and several inches taller than me and he did not like being made fun of. His jokes turned to physical threats. I began walking faster and then it happened.

My oldest brother, Jason, who had been walking about ten feet in front of me on our way to the locker room—after hearing every threat—suddenly slammed his pads and helmet down on the asphalt, turned around and got into this guy's face. "If you want to fight my brother, you're gonna have to fight me first!" I was speechless and in shock. For the first time ever, I stood proudly behind my oldest brother as the other guy slowly walked away with a look of astonishment on his face. Jason turned and picked up his helmet and shoulder pads and walked into the locker room without saying a word to me.

Lying in bed that night, I wept silent tears of joy. This day marked the first time my big brother, let alone anyone else, ever stood up for me. As I lay there in the dark, a seed of acceptance was planted inside me, and I began to let go of all the anger and bitterness I had bottled up over the years towards Jason. I had experienced so much rejection that I needed a breakthrough. I needed someone—anyone—to accept me without condition. I needed someone other than my mother to look beyond my many faults—my stutter, my chipped tooth—and simply love me for me. To my surprise, God used the person I secretly looked up to the most.

As a result of God using Jason that day, my life changed forever. The cloud of shame and embarrassment that once shadowed my every step was replaced with a rainbow of self-confidence and pride.

A seed of confidence was planted within me.

My newly increased confidence level had both positive and negative effects on my character. I began to walk and talk with my head held high, my chest out, and I even lost my stutter. But on the other hand, seeds of arrogance were planted inside me, as I began to show signs of cockiness—not only when it came to comparing my athletic ability to others, but also when it came to girls. It is truly amazing to think that what started out as a single kiss at the age of twelve had, by the end of my junior year in high school, escalated to receiving sexual favors from girls on a regular basis. Upon entering my senior year in high school, I finally quenched my thirst for intercourse.

I threw away my virginity because of my growing curiosity. I mean the way everyone talked about sex, I thought I was missing out on something special. I clearly remember thinking: *I can't believe it, I just lost my virginity! And for what? Yeah, it felt good, but that wasn't even worth the two minutes it took.*

Having sex may have silenced all of my critics and relieved me from the pressure from my buddies, but it also cultivated the seed of lust within me. Watered by my growing desire for intimacy, its roots threatened to destroy my soul. Leading up to my first sexual experience I thought: *Would it kill me to ignore all of the jokes and pressure from the fellas and wait until I get married to have sex? Does it mean that I am gay because I'm seventeen years old and haven't had sex yet?* Knowing the answer to both of those questions was no, why did I allow all of the pressure to get to me? After all, my dreams were beginning to come true.

Following my last high school football season, I received a full athletic scholarship to attend the greatest university in the country—the University of Michigan! So there I was, finally beginning to receive the admiration and respect I had always longed for. However, the only thing I longed for after having intercourse for the first time was more of the same. My ever-growing desire for sex ultimately overshadowed the little boy inside of me who for years longed for unconditional love.

CHAPTER 3
GOD ANSWERS PRAYER

What I failed to realize when I signed a "letter of intent" with the University of Michigan during my senior year in high school was that I was not *guaranteed* a scholarship. Signing the letter simply meant the university would *reserve* me a scholarship to attend their educational institution. Nevertheless, I got caught up in the hype and chose to adopt a careless and casual nature toward my academics, which nearly cost me the opportunity to achieve my childhood dream.

After signing my letter of intent, my mother beamed with pride! She would soon have not one, not two, but three sons attending Division 1A collegiate institutions on full athletic scholarships. God was truly answering her prayers. One day after I arrived home from school, I found Lloyd Carr, the head coach of the University of Michigan football program, sitting on my living room couch. *Wow, he must be really excited about me coming to play for Michigan.* After I greeted him and my mother, I took a seat on the edge of the couch next to my future head coach. My mother walked slowly out of the kitchen towards Coach Carr with one of her hands behind her back. She reached that hand out, passing a small white sheet of paper to Coach Carr.

"Here you go, Mr. Carr," she said. "I wanted you to take a look at Ian's most recent report card."

After taking a look at my grades, he turned to me and said, "Now look, Ian, I decided to give you a scholarship to come to the University of Michigan to be a *student*-athlete. If you don't improve these grades, I will not hesitate to take your scholarship away and give it to somebody else."

I could feel myself slowly sliding back into the couch. I knew exactly why my grades were suffering—I was too busy chasing girls. While informing my future head coach about my below-average grades might have been a bit extreme, my mother had no choice. I *needed* this wake-up call. After commenting on my grades, Coach Carr rose to his feet to leave. I thanked him for taking the time to visit. Following his exit, I sat back down on the couch in silence. *Man! Mom is not playin'. But doesn't she know that I could lose my scholarship because of what she just did?* God was clearly using my mother to teach me a valuable life lesson. As I got up and headed for my bedroom, my mother said, "You are going to have to learn how to finish! I don't care if you do have a scholarship waiting for you! If you keep bringing home grades like this, you won't have a scholarship because you failed to *finish* high school strong!"

I made the decision then and there to focus on finishing the remainder of my senior year as strongly as I possibly could.

I thought, *I can hold off on chasing girls until I graduate—then I'm off to college!*

When the time for me to leave for college arrived, I was indeed the happiest person in the world. Even though my mother lived only twenty minutes away from where I attended college—I was free.

Since the days of riding in the car as a child and my mother challenging my brothers and me with the question, *"What do you want to be when you grow up?"*, I had always dreamed of attending the University of Michigan. In fact, during the time my mother attended the university, I routinely hopped on the free transit bus just to ride around the campus. It was beautiful. Walking the streets of downtown Ann Arbor made my dream of going to college there tangible. I loved watching people with their backpacks full of books on their way to class, or on their way to study. I observed students eating lunch beneath the deciduous trees that shaded the green lawns of central campus. I took it all in. I often visualized myself walking to class on one of Michigan's beautiful summer or fall days—and spending the winters on a distant tropical island! Achieving my childhood dream of attending the University of Michigan watered the seed of faith within me.

Upon my arrival to campus in the summer of 1996, Ann Arbor already felt like home. After getting settled into my dorm room, it didn't take long to realize having a full athletic scholarship would be both a blessing and a curse. While I had been given an opportunity to further my education, there are no degrees handed out for chasing women.

After losing my virginity during my final year of high school, by the time my freshmen year of college got underway, an awful seed of promiscuity had been planted inside me—as I had already had sex with five girls. Before I knew it, I had jumped onto the fast track toward becoming a womanizer. It was as if I was trying to make up for all the times my brothers had shunned me and the guys from high school had teased me for being a virgin. I could still feel the sharp pain of rejection and loneliness. *But I'm not lonely anymore,* I thought. *No one is rejecting me now. Everybody loves me and I can get any girl I want. Now who's laughing?* I took advantage of every opportunity I could to be with a woman, no matter the time or place—in my dorm room with my roommate in his bed right next to me, in a woman's dorm room with her roommate lying in her bed right next to us, in the middle of the day, before practice, after practice, the night before a big exam, even during two-a-days—the period right before the football season begins, when coaches attempt to isolate players in order to keep them focused on football. At the time, my thinking was simply: *I'm only gonna be in college once, so I might as well live it up!*

I was so busy chasing women I hardly noticed my character and personality changing for the worse. Roots from the seed of arrogance began to consume my heart and mind. The pure and innocent little boy who for years struggled with issues of rejection and loneliness now found himself fighting to keep his place within me. My arrogance exhibited itself in strolling into class fifteen minutes late, or in the way I began addressing, and undressing, women. I felt as though I were invincible. In fact, I had become so arrogant that after missing a class for an entire semester, I had the audacity to show up for the final exam, believing my professor would give me a passing grade. I remember strutting into the lecture hall and taking a final exam from the professor. Hearing her chuckle under her breath, I asked, "Oh, you're going to fail me?" When she nodded her head yes, I handed the exam back to her and pompously walked out of the lecture hall.

The truth was that I completed just enough of my class work and attended barely enough of my classes to remain eligible to play football—or so I thought. Had my grades been based on playing football and chasing girls, I would have been on the dean's list every semester. I was in need of yet another wake up call. After performing extremely poorly academically during my first two semesters of college, just as my third semester got underway, I received a random and unexpected request to meet with my head coach.

"The Director of Undergraduate Admissions, Ted Spencer, wants to speak with you," Coach Carr said, handing me the dean's address.

"Okay. About what?"

"You'll find out when you get there!" he sharply replied.

Upon arriving at the dean's office, he invited me in and offered me a seat.

"So, Ian, how are you doing with your classes?" he asked. "Are you handling the class workload okay?"

"Yes, sir!" I responded. "I got off to a little bit of a rough start, but I'll get it together. I'm going to do better this semester."

"Well, you actually don't have a choice," he replied. "You see, Ian, at the end of each semester I receive a list of all the students who are not performing well academically. As a result of your grades from your second semester, unfortunately you are on the list, which means you are now on academic probation. I hate to be the bearer of bad news, but if you are on academic probation for two consecutive semesters, you will lose your scholarship." My stomach dropped to the floor. I thought about my mother and how disappointed she would be. *I just got here!* I thought. *I'm not about to be kicked out!*

Needless to say, I put forth greater effort and improved my grades tremendously. However, that was not my last meeting with my coaches, academic advisors, or the dean regarding my grades. One of the biggest challenges during my freshmen year was time management. Between women, playing football, and all of the partying, it was tough to find time for my class work and studying—as a seed of procrastination was planted within me. I procrastinated all the time, consistently waiting until the last minute to complete papers or study for exams. In fact, I probably set a record for all-nighters. During one off-season, after having reconstructive shoulder surgery and being doped up on painkillers, I left the hospital and went straight to the "fish bowl"—the computer lab on Michigan's central campus—to begin writing a ten-page term paper that was due the next day. Glued to my seat for the entire night, I typed my entire paper with one hand, finishing about seven o'clock the next morning.

During those days, I also spent a great deal of time reflecting on the difficult journey I traveled in order to get to college. In the midst of all the partying and the sex, these periods of reflection helped me remain determined to finish my college degree. Painful images of being all alone, kneeling in my room, hugging myself, and whispering prayers to God as tears streamed down my face, often watered my "deep-seeded" feelings of rejection and loneliness. There were many nights I sought ways to break the chain of hurt, hoping I could leave the painful memories from my childhood behind.

One night in my freshman year, while getting ready for bed, my dorm room phone rang. It was around midnight. When I answered the phone, I heard the voice of my older brother, Jeremy, on the other end. He was weeping and sobbing as he spoke, "Ian, I'm sorry for everything I did to you growing up—all the pain and hurt I caused you. I'm calling to ask you to forgive me!"

As I stood there holding the phone, I froze. *How could I ever forgive you for tearing out my heart on the basketball court that day on the hill?* Deep inside of me I still held onto the anger I felt toward Jeremy when he stood up for my cousin instead of me. But, after being moved to compassion by his sincerity, I chose to forgive him. God used Jeremy's phone call to begin uprooting the seeds of anger, rejection and loneliness—breaking the chain that led back to my painful childhood. In that moment, I let go of my anger and bitterness towards him.

Being plagued by fumble-itis and missing the first four games of the season because of an injury to my foot, Jeremy's expression of love watered the seed of confidence within me. Soon after forgiving Jeremy, I found myself beginning to enjoy my freshmen year at Michigan.

In the four weeks it took my bruised foot to heal, I had plenty of time to become better acquainted with a new diversion—alcohol. Quickly life became one big party. Oddly enough, I didn't really care for the taste of alcohol, but I drank anyway. There were several nights I returned to my dorm room heavily intoxicated. Sometimes I would even drink until I passed out. Why did I drink? Well at the time, I wasn't strong enough to stand alone. Everyone else seemed to be doing it and fitting in was safe—it kept me from being ridiculed by my team- and classmates.

I remember going to a house party one night and, after getting wasted, I staggered back to my dorm room alone. As soon as my head touched my pillow, I passed out. I made the mistake of lying on my back, which nearly cost me my life. Waking up the next morning fully dressed and finding myself on the floor next to the trash can, I looked up and saw my roommate, Marcus Knight, a quiet southerner from Sylacauga, Alabama, sitting on the edge of his bed, rubbing his head.

"Maaan, how in the world did I end up on the floor?" I asked.

"When I walked into the room last night, you were on your back choking on your own throw-up, so I turned you over and helped you get on the floor to a trash can."

"What? I don't remember throwing up!"

"Well," he said, in a tone filled with anger and frustration, "if I didn't come back to the room last night, yo' a@@ might be dead right now. Don't do that sh#* no mo'!" After silently thanking God for sparing my life, I apologized to Marcus. I also thanked him for taking care of me the way he did. Even though I promised myself that night to never get drunk again, it would be a promise I would break many times over. While Marcus did not speak to me for a few days, he finally forgave me for what took place that night.

A week or so after my near-death experience, I heard an account of two college students who died in their sleep by choking on their own vomit due to being intoxicated. Needless to say, I took a break from alcohol after hearing the news of their deaths—but it was short lived.

Partying became a way of life for me. For the remainder of my freshmen year I found myself in the same routine: partying, chasing women, and playing football. After missing the first four games of the season, my foot healed and I hit the field running full speed. I was originally recruited as a running back, but I only got to play on special teams my freshman year. Every time we kicked-off or punted the football to our opponents, I found myself trying to punish players on the opposing team. In fact, I did such a great job of hitting and tackling on special teams as a freshman that, as I entered the team meeting room for our first full team meeting of my sophomore year, after looking for my notebook on the offensive side of the room, one of the coaches commented, "Oh Ian, your notebook is over there on the defensive side of the room."

I walked across the room, scanning the notebooks for my name. Finally, I saw my name on a notebook that had LINEBACKERS on the cover in bold print. Shocked, I immediately thought, *I know Coach Carr did NOT change my position to linebacker without asking me! I don't tackle and hit people; I score touchdowns!* But that's exactly what Coach did. I did not hear one word he spoke during that entire meeting; my mind was consumed with anger and frustration. As soon as the meeting ended, I walked into Coach Carr's office.

"So what's going on? Why did you change my position?"

"Well, Ian," he said, "after evaluating your performance on special teams from last season and this past spring, I decided to move you to the defensive side of the ball."

"Well, I don't want to be a linebacker," I protested. "I have never played defense in my life—other than a few plays here and there in high school."

"Well, look," he replied firmly, "I told you when you came here that I would give you a shot to play tailback and I gave you a shot. Now I want to see how you perform at linebacker."

Unhappy with his justification for changing my position—and being angry with him—I left his office and went to my first meeting as a linebacker. At the time, I was living with my mom's best friend from college—Shabnum Sheikh—who kindly offered me the basement of her home, which was located within walking distance to campus. When I got back to her house after practice, I was pissed to say the least! So I called my mother.

"Mom, they switched me to linebacker!"

"Well," she said, "just try linebacker out and see if you like the position."

"Mom, I am a running back!" I replied, "They recruited me as a running back and now they switch my position without even asking me? I want to transfer to another school."

"Wait a minute. You need to look at the bright side," she said with love and conviction, "and thank God for giving you the ability and versatility to play multiple positions."

She made a great point. And even though I was displeased, I made up my mind to give this new position my very best. Once I began to grasp the concept, I found myself feeling more and more comfortable on the defensive side of the line of scrimmage. I felt like a lion that had finally been un-caged!

Then came the day of our first full-padded practice. *No matter what,* I thought, *just go out there today and hit somebody!* Shortly after practice began, the whistle blew and everyone started getting riled up for "nine-on-seven"—the only *live* hitting drill during practice. Following the starting defenses domination of the second team offense, my linebacker coach, Jim Hermann, sent me in with the second defensive unit to face the starting offensive team. This being my first day going live and having no clue as to how to read offensive keys or where to align, I thought, *When the ball snaps just run and hit somebody as hard as you can!*

As the back-up quarterback, *a guy named Tom*, began shouting his cadence—"Blue 52, Blue 52"—I crouched down into the stance I had learned just a few days prior. I locked the fullback into my sights. As the center snapped the ball, all I could think was, *GO!* Without any concern for the ball carrier, I ran directly toward the fullback. As we collided like two freight trains, his helmet flew off! When I saw his helmet rolling on the ground and the completely stunned look on his face, I unleashed a huge roar. The entire defense went bananas.

They all came over and jumped on top of me, as if to say, *We welcome you as a member of our defense*—a pride of hungry lions.

At that moment, on the green practice fields of Schembechler Hall, a seed of intimidation was planted inside me, as I became an offensive coordinator's worst nightmare—a defensive linebacker! *Well, well, well,* I thought, *it turns out Coach Carr does know a thing or two about football.* Later that year, our football team, led by Charles Woodson and Brian Griese, two men I greatly respect, went on to win the National Championship. To this day, Coach Carr, who has proved to be an even better human being than a head coach, still reminds me who's responsible for my move to linebacker. As he jokingly says, "Now look, Gold, you owe me!"

Once I settled into my new position, I also found myself wanting to settle down off the field as well. During my sophomore year, I decided to find one woman to spend time with. With that I entered into my first, and last, committed relationship during college—it quickly came to an end, as the seed of promiscuity received water. After cheating on her during our first summer break away from each other, I felt so guilty that I told her all the details of what happened. I felt awful about hurting her. She forgave me, but never trusted me again.

I decided from then on that I would tell women up front that I did not want to be in a committed relationship—I just wanted to have fun. This noncommittal pattern lasted for the remainder of my time at Michigan. I believed that as long as I was honest and told women the truth, no one would get hurt. Any woman interested in spending time with me had to agree to my terms and conditions. Sadly, there were plenty of women who were willing to let me have my way. But I felt empty. Sure I spent lots of time in college with beautiful and intellectual women, but the feeling of emptiness surfaced each time they would get out of my bed to leave. I couldn't understand why I felt a void. *I'm living the life I used to dream of as a kid, so why do I feel like this? I've forgiven my older brothers and I really don't care if I ever talk to my dad again—so what is it? Maybe God is trying to tell me something. Maybe there will always be a void until I make a decision to surrender my life to Christ?*

Unlike the usual saying, "at the end of the day,"—at the *beginning* of the day, I had been born and raised in holiness, which meant I should do my best to obey God's word and commandments. My mother, in many ways, expressed to me that God would not be pleased with me if I failed to obey His commandments and laws. So despite feeling guilty from all the sex and the partying—at times I would still make the trip to Ypsilanti to attend Sunday service. Seated in the same sanctuary in which my mother pleaded to the saints to pray for me as a child, I was now in far more need of their prayers. As seeds of lust, arrogance and promiscuity, replaced the seeds of anger, rejection, and loneliness that I battled to overcome as a child. Each time I visited Mount Olive, Pastor Willie Sheard would greet my teammates and me with a warm welcome. I remember one day he said, "Young men, you can achieve anything you want to in this life so long as you keep the Lord first in your lives. So reach for the stars. The sky is the limit to what you can achieve with the Lord!"

I greatly appreciated his words of encouragement, but following his remarks I heard God say, "But if you reach for heaven, you will leave the stars far behind!" Upon hearing God's words, a small seed of hope was planted within my embattled soul. Sadly, however, I found myself losing the fight for my soul as I sped down the path of unrighteousness. While attending Sunday services, even though I received praises from members of the congregation for my accomplishments, I felt extremely unworthy. *I'm such a hypocrite. If people knew the real me they wouldn't praise me—they'd rebuke me and pour blessed oil on me, all while praying for my salvation and deliverance from sin.*

Despite being taught holiness all my life and my occasional visits to Sunday service, I still bounced back and forth between college girls. And quickly learned how having sex outside of marriage—with or without protection—can result in painful and embarrassing consequences.

One night at a party, a girl who lived in a neighboring dormitory, and also dated one of my teammates, expressed her interest in me. I took her back to my dorm room where we were intimate. In the weeks that followed, the situation got really messy—my teammate found out about our affair. What made the situation even worse was that I contracted an STD—"crabs". I felt dirty! *How could I use protection and still get an STD?* I wondered. I had to disinfect my entire room—clothes, sheets, and even my mattress.

From then on, I was determined to be more selective of the women with whom I chose to be intimate. STDs can frighten even the toughest people. I often said to myself, *I'm not hooking up with her because she looks like she might have an STD.* Or, *I don't have to use protection with her because she's too fine to have an STD.* In the end, I was wrong and foolish to think this way. I acted as if being young, careless, and athletically gifted, meant that I was supposed to live dangerously and flirt with death. Needless to say, I was in constant need of prayer.

Throughout college, there were several specific occasions I thought about my mother and how she would feel if she knew about how I was living. There were actually times I could feel her prayers for God's protection over me. In fact, while standing in my dorm room one day, I felt a strong sense of my mother praying for me. Out of my curiosity, I decided to pick up the phone and find out if my intuition was correct. After my mother picked up the phone, I said, "Mom, are you praying for me right now?"

"Yeah," she replied.

In that moment, a seed of peace was planted inside me. As I became confident that regardless of the number of parties I attended, the number of women I chased, or the amount of alcohol I consumed, my mother would not cease to pray for God's protection over my life—whether or not I believed I needed it. In fact, if it were not for God answering my mother's prayers, I probably would not be here today.

CHAPTER 4
A WHOLE NEW WORLD

I had always dreamed of being a professional athlete and, shortly after the clock expired on my college experience, that dream became a reality. The Denver Broncos selected me with their second pick in the 2000 NFL Draft. As my mother, brothers, my ex-girlfriend, and I anxiously watched the NFL Draft in the living room of the small house my mother was renting, the phone rang and everyone fell silent. My mother picked up the phone and then silently handed it to me. I heard the voice of the Broncos head coach, Mike Shanahan, a man for whom I have profound respect, say, "Hey, Ian, do you want to be a Denver Bronco?"

"Yes, sir!"

"Okay, we're getting ready to draft you. Welcome to the Broncos."

Hanging up the phone, I shared the unofficial news with my family. Seconds later, the announcer at the podium on TV said, "And with the fortieth pick of the 2000 NFL Draft, the Denver Broncos select defensive linebacker Ian Gold from the University of Michigan!" Once we heard the official announcement my family and I embraced. As the phone calls from family, friends, and media started flooding in, I thought to myself, *I really did it!* In spite of all of the heartache, all the loneliness and rejection, all the anger and frustration I struggled with up until this point in my life's journey, I stood proudly above all of it that day, saying loudly, *You didn't destroy me! You couldn't make me give up! I beat you!*

Achieving, yet, another one of my childhood dreams watered the growing seed of faith within me.

Following the draft, God used a select few individuals to plant valuable seeds of wisdom inside me. My strength and conditioning coach from the University of Michigan, Mike Gittleson, was one of the first. During one of my last workouts with him just *before* I was drafted, I remember telling Mike, "You wouldn't believe some of the guys at the NFL combine who already have luxury cars and jewelry—and the draft hasn't even been held yet."

I will never forget his reply to me: "Ian, listen to me and always remember this—a hungry man works ten times harder than a well fed man! Stay hungry!"

Mike's words of wisdom had an immediate and lasting impact on my attitude, as they challenged and motivated me to never allow my success, or failure, no matter how great or small, determine my work ethic. But he wasn't the only one.

As I sat in my Aunt Sis's kitchen one day, she said, "Now let me tell you, you're going to have a whole lot of people saying, 'Hey Ian, you better make sure you don't let all of that money change you,' and—," she paused, "you make sure you tell them, 'Okay I won't change. But, you make sure you don't let it change you either. You didn't ask me for anything before, so don't ask me for anything now." As she finished, I began laughing, realizing she made a very valid point about something I was soon to experience.

Regardless of how much wisdom I received, I had to learn a number of lessons the hard way. As a result of my instant fame and fortune, I began losing a sense of reality. I began to lose what hold I had left on good morals and values after graduating from college. Seeds of invincibility and indestructibility were planted inside me, and sadly, each day I became more and more unrecognizable to myself.

At the time I was drafted, I still did not "do titles" with women. In other words, no woman had ownership of me—even though all sorts of women started offering me ridiculous and outrageous propositions. For instance, shortly after Draft Day I received a phone call from a woman I had dated during the summer before my freshmen year of college.

"Hey Ian, can we talk?" she asked. "There are a few things I would like to say to you, but I'd like to see you in person."

Not having seen her for years and being curious about what she wanted to say, I invited her to come over to my mother's house.

During a short walk around the quiet, tree-filled neighborhood, she asked, "Well, I know we haven't been together for years now and I know you're leaving town, but I just wanted to know if we could sleep together one last time?"

Shocked by her boldness and forwardness—which turned out to be modest compared to women I met in subsequent years—I politely thanked her for her offer and declined. This encounter was the first time I had ever sensed complete desperation from a woman. For the first time in my life, I feared the motives and intentions of a woman—but it certainly wouldn't be the last. Over the years I've come to realize that just as a majority of young men battle against the need to be validated by their peers, young women are also fighting an internal battle. Dating back to Eve in the Garden of Eden, all women have been born with a power to influence men—a power, which they can use for either good or evil.

Therefore, girls need to be taught at a young age how to control their ability to influence the opposite sex—keeping their powers of influence subjected to the spirit of God. Sadly, if they do not learn how to win this battle, by the time they become young women, the devil will use them for his evil purposes. In Ephesians 6:12, the Apostle Paul says,

> *For we wrestle not against flesh and blood, but against principalities, against powers, against the rulers of the*

darkness of this world, against spiritual wickedness in high places.

One look at today's media and Internet is all it takes to see spiritual wickedness—as sex sells not only music and other products, but also the idea of an entire lifestyle centered on million dollar cribs and luxury vehicles. You see, upon entering the NFL, unbeknownst to me, the devil knew exactly how to make me weak. In Proverbs chapter thirty-one, King Lemuel's mother gave him a list of instructions. A portion of her instructions reads as follows:

Give not thy strength unto women, nor thy ways to that which destroyeth Kings. (Proverbs 31:3)

The more I became involved in improper sexual relationships with women, the weaker I became spiritually. And unfortunately, my growing spiritual weakness made it quite easy to be seduced and persuaded by ungodly women. At the time, by simply "showing some skin", or displaying their sexy curves in a sensual or seductive manner women could get me to do whatever they wanted me to do.

I'm *not* saying women are responsible for the lack of self-control that I exhibited. What I am saying is women should be mindful of the way they carry themselves around men, just as men need to begin acknowledging women for far more than their physical attributes. Women should *demand* to be treated with respect and dignity. Sadly, however, when young girls grow up to become attention-starved, half-naked cheerleaders bouncing up and down in front of crowds of men, they resemble many of the strippers I—inexcusably—tipped throughout my entire NFL career. Therefore, it is my responsibility to teach my daughter at a young age about the power of influence she possesses. So, by the time she becomes a young woman, she will use her power of influence for the purpose and cause of Christ Jesus.

Being childless at the time, however, and giving no thought to the little eyes that would soon be watching my every move, I entered my first season in the NFL having little regard for women—or myself. With no more classes and grades to worry about, my sole focus became playing football to the best of my ability—and chasing women! When I arrived in Denver I had zero self-control. It also didn't help that a number of my teammates were in a similar place in their lives.

Think of it this way: *Young men + six, seven, or eight figure salaries + four months off each year + NFL status and fame = one hot mess!*

Most of the time, when a young man is given a truck load of money, four months off of work each year, and the status that comes from playing in the NFL—it'll be virtually impossible for him to use his time and resources constructively. I was certainly no exception and I was presented with a number of new adventures and challenges. Of all the vices available for me to try: gambling, women, drugs, and alcohol, I think it's safe to say you know the one I chose—women. When I arrived in Denver, I took full advantage of every opportunity to party—nightclubs, bars, and especially strip clubs. During one of my first nights out clubbing, I noticed a beautiful woman standing a short distance away from me. Having all of the right curves—her jeans skin-tight and hair a mile long down her back—I switched into hunting mode and set out for the chase. But, the chase ended rather quickly.

"I'm with him," she commented, as she motioned across the large nightclub. When I turned to look at the man she was looking at, I saw one of my teammates standing alone. This puzzled me even more, because I knew he had a wife and kids.

Before I continue any further, let me pause to say that contrary to popular belief, not every male professional athlete is a womanizer. By the end of my professional football career I came to know a number of athletes who were loyal, committed, and faithful to their wives—men dedicated to their families, who did not believe in going to strip clubs, or paying for sex—men who I respected and admired for their loyalty and commitment to their wives.

Now back to the nightclub.

Later that night, I stood next to that teammate and we both admired his mistress from a distance.

"She's sexy, ain't she?" he said.

"Yeah, she is," I replied. "So hey, aren't you married?"

"Man, look. I told my wife that she could either go marry a trash man who's gonna cheat on her and be broke, or she could be with me and have everything she's ever wanted and dreamed of—and be cheated on. She chose to stay with me."

I was completely lost for words. *Did he just say what I think he said?* My brief conversation with him turned out to be an introduction to *a whole new world.* A world in which there appeared to be no rules, no boundaries, and no guidelines for any of us athletes. It seemed we could do whatever, whenever, with whomever we wished without any serious consequences—or so I thought! While my sleeping with a different woman every other night may have been in poor taste, in some crazy way I convinced myself that my teammate—who was cheating on his wife—was much worse. He was up for the Scum of the Year award because, after all, he broke his marital vows. My situation was different, I thought. What I failed to realize, however, was that if he earned first place for his mistreatment of his wife, I was the runner-up! Despite my thoughts and judgments of him and the "other woman" from the club that night, eventually I would begin a sexual relationship with her—one that spanned the next year or more.

Unbeknownst to me, hearing my teammate's comments on this particular night resulted in me gaining a *false* sense of righteousness—as I thought, *Wow, I know I'm righteous compared to him because I'm not married with kids.* Little did I know, however, that I was *far* from being righteous

The truth is: the *only* measure I should have used to calculate or determine my righteousness was Jesus Christ. In hindsight, had I measured my unrighteousness up against Jesus' holiness and righteousness—instead of the sinful and wicked nature of the men and women surrounding me—the root of my sexual obsession would have been destroyed.

That wasn't the case, however.

Unfortunately, my growing sense of "false righteousness" made me believe that I loved God—after all, my sinful actions were not as bad as others. The truth is, however, that as I succeeded at breaking God's commandments and laws, I failed miserably at loving Him.

While I never used drugs, by the end of my rookie season womanizing had become my drug. The adrenaline rush I got from competing with a room full of men to win the attention of the most attractive woman there had become much more than just a game—it was an addiction. I couldn't go more than a few days without it, and being so consumed caused me to make poor decisions that I would never before had dreamed of making. For instance, there were times I had sex with two or three women in the same day, thinking, *I've come this far, I might as well keep going.* As a result, there were times that I slept with four or five women in the same day. My obsession with chasing women led me into the deepest, darkest shark-infested waters.

After purchasing a small townhouse in a quiet neighborhood near the Broncos' training facility, I found myself living the life I had only seen and heard about in movies and music videos. I would go to nightclubs with one question in mind: *Who am I going to take home tonight?* Many times, I found myself heading back to my townhouse with a woman after only being in a club for twenty minutes.

Sure, I enjoyed a challenge every once and a while—having to engage in an intellectual conversation with a woman, or take a woman out on a fancy date. At the end of the day, however, it came down to one thought: *I hope she wants to have sex.* Growing tired of wining and dining women, I began to purchase pornographic videos and magazines so I could pleasure myself. I also paid women for sex on occasion. I found watching porn and paying for sex to be a way to fulfill my ever-growing sexual appetite without having to chase. I wasted thousands of dollars on magazines, videos, and paying women for sex—until finally, while surfing the Internet one day, I found a free pornographic website. Now needing only an Internet connection, my sexual appetite grew exponentially. My obsession with sex reached a level that if a woman spent the night at my house and did not want to have sex, I would either kick her out, or pleasure myself lying right next to her—then roll over and go to sleep.

During this period of my life I became a regular at nearly every strip club in town. In fact, I had gotten to know a security guard at one local strip club so well that he would let me know when new, attractive women started working at the club. Women in strip clubs became no different than women I met in bars or nightclubs. In fact, I actually preferred meeting women in strip clubs rather than nightclubs or bars because I could take a look at the complete package before I brought it home. I also didn't have to spend the time wining and dining them to get what I wanted. The nights I found myself bored—or maybe in a fight with one of the women with whom I had a so-called committed relationship—I wouldn't hesitate picking up a woman from a strip club to let go of my worries and cares through sex.

In 2005, I actually had serious thoughts of dating an exotic dancer I met after moving to Tampa, Florida. While seated alone in one of Tampa's popular strip clubs, onto the dance stage walked a stunningly beautiful woman. Her entire being said SEX—from the red see-through outfit she had on to her perfectly sculpted Italian physique underneath it. For the remainder of the evening, I became the hunter and she the prey. Following her performance, she glided across the room to thank me for the tip I had given her. When she took a seat I complimented her beauty and in a subtle way let her know what I did for a living.

A few days later we were in my bathtub.

From that point forward, whenever she drove from the east coast of Florida—where she lived at the time—to the west coast to work a few nights at the club, we had sex. Our sexual relationship would stretch over the next four years.

The first time I paid for sex was during a weekend of partying in Detroit. As I partied the night away, I met a number of women who, unfortunately, had other plans for the night. As I sat in my hotel room alone, knowing there were strippers all over the hotel, I thought, *I could pay one of those girls for sex and go to sleep satisfied. Or I can be sexually frustrated all night!* I got up and went downstairs, picked out the exotic dancer I wanted, came to an agreement on a price and then we went back up to my room. After she left my room I sat on the edge of the bed in disbelief that I just paid a woman to have sex with me! I thought of the many stories I had heard from other guys. Once again, I somehow convinced myself that my actions were nothing compared to what they were doing.

When I look back on this part of my journey, it's natural to ask why: Why did I pay for sex, pornographic magazines and movies, and evenings at strip clubs? I used to tell my buddies—and even some of the women I casually spent time with—that I could not spend more than two consecutive days with the same woman. And sure enough, every two days the revolving door would turn and as one woman exited, another one entered. If I ever found myself spending more than two days with the same woman I would become extremely irritable, which naturally caused them to want to go home. In the end, paying for sex, pornography, and frequenting strip clubs became a way for me to break up the monotony of being with the same woman.

Now you may be wondering why, if I knew it was wrong, did I continue to do it? That's a good question. You see, at that time my lifestyle and my career moved at such a fast pace, I became completely *reactive* to everything around me. In the same way that I learned to think and react quickly to whatever the offense did on the football field and reviewing my mistakes later, so too in my life off the field, I began carelessly reacting, making senseless choices and decisions. I would have sex with a woman and think, *Ian, why did you talk her into having sex with you when you know you don't ever want to see her again?* The truth was that, although struggling inwardly, outwardly I told women whatever they wanted to hear in order to get them into my bed. I found myself constantly convicted during this period of my life, often thinking—before, during, or after having sex—*I know God is not pleased with my actions.* But I didn't want to think about that, as I went to great lengths to hide my sexual indiscretions from others.

CHAPTER 5
DECEPTION

To my family and friends, my supporters and fans, I appeared to be a decent man with a kind heart. However, there were not many who knew the man I transformed into after the crowds went home, the lights dimmed, and the cameras were turned off. Admittedly, upon the completion of my rookie season in the NFL, I was nothing more than a professional womanizer. Due to my childhood experiences, I thought having respect for women meant not verbally or physically abusing them like my dad did my mother. I often thought, *At least I'm not like my dad! I don't put my hands on women. I'm not an adulterer—and I'm certainly not an alcoholic.* Since I didn't want to run the risk of ruining my professional career—and also to not be like my dad—I made the decision to stop drinking during my second year with the Broncos. I was proud of myself for this and I somehow convinced myself that the rest of my behavior didn't resemble my dad's at all. But the reality was that, with each passing day, I became more like the man I both feared and loved as a child.

At the end of my second professional season in February of 2002, football fans, my peers, coaches from around the league, and the media voted me to the Pro Bowl! Filled with excitement, I phoned my mother and brothers and told them to pack their bags for Hawaii! Yet in the midst of all the excitement, all I was really thinking about were the beautiful Hawaiian women. In Honolulu, I connected with another player whose flight arrived around the same time as mine. Leaving the airport and heading to our hotel, we were both thinking the same thing: *Where are all of the Hawaiian beauties?*

Later that same evening, with my family not arriving for another day or so, the other player and I set out together like a pair of male lions combing the plains of an unconquered territory. Though the first night in Hawaii ended up being pretty uneventfully for me, it was a different story altogether for my buddy.

When we met up for breakfast the next morning he looked as if someone had just died.

"Dude, you won't believe what happened to me last night." He told me that, after hiring the services of a prostitute, he didn't realize that his cell phone had inadvertently redialed his girlfriend's phone number. His girlfriend heard all of the steamy details he and the woman-for-hire discussed in the back of the limousine. Shortly thereafter, his phone rang. It was his girlfriend calling him back to give him a piece of her mind and to end their relationship.

"Man, that sucks," I said, shaking my head.

"I'm thinking about going home," he remarked.

I sat listening to him for the next thirty minutes as he looked and sounded worse and worse. After we finished breakfast, other players began arriving at the hotel. Following a brief team meeting later that evening, about ten of us hopped in a few limousines and headed to a small bar in Waikiki. When we arrived I noticed a group of Hawaiian women walking up to the door. One of them caught my eye. As we entered the bar together, the group of women decided to join us. Seated amidst a starving pack of male wolves, I thought: *If I don't make a move on her, somebody else will!* She was by far the most beautiful one out of the entire group.

As she finished eating her sandwich, I asked, "Hey, you wanna go talk over there where it's not so crowded and noisy?"

"Sure," she responded.

Just as I got up to follow her one of the guys whispered, "Man, I was just about to—"

"Too late!" I said, cutting him off before he could even finish his sentence.

She and I began to talk at the empty bar. In addition to being one of the most beautiful women I had ever been in the company of, I also found her to be one of the most intriguing women I had ever met. I even pinched myself at one point during my encounter with her, just to make sure I wasn't dreaming.

We talked about our faith in God. We talked about our appreciation for family. After talking with her for nearly an hour I had clearly fallen in lust, and for the moment I thought, *I'm in love.* Spending time with her made me feel intoxicated, which greatly impaired my judgment. Finally full from our conversation, we decided to rejoin the others. When I took a seat next to one of my buddies, he asked, "Damn! You gon' let her come up for air?"

"Nah," I said arrogantly.

Soon after our return, everyone decided to leave and go to a nightclub down the street, but having other plans in our minds, we parted ways with them. Out of sheer ignorance, I made an extremely careless decision—I went back to her hotel room.

Despite the connection I felt with her, I became a bit uneasy when we arrived at her hotel room. *I just finished my second year in the league and made it to my first Pro Bowl. I've got a bright and promising career ahead of me and I'm about to risk it all for one night with her? What if this is all a set up and I get robbed or killed?*

She said, "Hey, I'm going to take a quick shower."

And with that, all my apprehensions were chucked out of the hotel window! I got undressed and under the covers quicker than a fireman. When she re-emerged from the bathroom, wearing only a white towel, we were intimate. Intoxicated by her beauty, I didn't use any protection. I made one dumb decision after the other. *Man, she could have an STD,* I thought. But, taking one more look at her, I dismissed my thought—*Nah, she's way too beautiful!*

After taking a shower together, she offered to drive me to the stadium the next morning for my first practice, so I stayed the night. Awakened by the sunlight, I rolled over and saw her beautiful face. *Wow!* Seconds later, however, I realized I had overslept! Somehow my alarm clock failed to go off. I began to panic. *I'm at my first Pro Bowl. It's the first day of practice, and I'm late!* The drive to the stadium felt like a roller coaster—and my stomach just wanted it all to stop! I thought: *I'll just walk out to the practice field with her and say, "Now is she not the most beautiful excuse in the world for me being late for practice?"* It didn't take long to decide that approach probably wouldn't work.

We arrived at the stadium and just before I got out of the car, she handed me a photo of her that was on her dashboard. Following a kiss goodbye, I assured her I would see her after practice. As I hurried into the locker room, sure enough, my teammates had already gotten dressed and were out on the practice field! My nerves began to settle down as I thought about the situation. *Dude! Why am I trippin'? This is the Pro Bowl! No one should be uptight because I'm late. After all, we're here to have a good time!*

After putting on my cleats and grabbing my helmet, I jogged onto the practice field and my head coach, Bill

Cowher, a coach for whom I had tremendous respect, walked up to me and said, "Okay, Gold, why were you late?"

"Coach, I'm really sorry," I explained, "my stupid alarm clock didn't go off and I overslept."

He responded with a smile. "I'm glad you're having a good time, Gold, but let's not make this a habit."

I got the message and thanked him for his understanding. After he walked away, Rodney Harrison, a veteran player I respected, asked, "Ian! What do you do for a living?"

"Uh, I'm a professional football player."

"Then be a professional, Ian! Be a *Pro*!" he said gravely.

While I knew he had a valid point and I appreciated him for taking the opportunity to make me aware of my lack of professionalism, my mind was still laying in bed with my Hawaiian beauty. *I can still smell her sweet scent,* I thought as I participated in the drills.

After practice, I walked into the locker room and a few guys started to give me a hard time for being late. Out of my arrogance, I placed her photo directly in the line of sight of one of my teammates. When the photo made its way around to a few of my teammates, one of them asked, "Damn! Is this why you were late? Hell, I would've been late too! She got any sisters?"

"Nope," I laughed.

"Well, why don't you throw her to the wolves and see if she'll come back!"

I laughed along with everyone else who heard the comical remark. But then it hit me, *Wait a minute. Dude, you're married!*

Strangely enough, his comment eliminated the guilt I felt from having sex with her on the first night we met, and for being late for practice. Every free moment I had during the remainder of my time in Hawaii, I spent with her. That night, after practice, we went out together. Pulling me out on the dance floor, she danced circles around me. Every person on the dance floor stopped to watch her. During a slow dance, she sang in my ear—she sounded like an angel. *Who is this woman? I know I just met her last night but I feel like I've known her my entire life!* In fact, when a teammate—the one who told me to "be a pro" on the practice field—saw her and I walking together outside of the hotel, he jokingly asked, "So, when is the wedding?"

Although I laughed his question off, it didn't sound like a bad idea to either of us. In fact, it quickly became a topic of conversation.

Due to all of the time I spent with her, I failed to spend the quality time that I should have with the people closest to me—my mother, three brothers, and my roommate from college, Marcus—who were all there to support me. As I look back now, sadly there were many periods during my career when I pushed my family members and close friends away. When I grew tired of wearing the mask that covered up my true identity—a womanizer—I isolated myself by completely closing off from the world. And in isolation I found myself losing more and more ground in the battle for my soul. There were many times I prayed, *Lord, I love you, but I just don't think I can stop having sex.* For many years, thoughts like this continued to prevent me from fully surrendering my life to the Lord.

After the Pro Bowl, I returned to Denver and the professional cheerleader who I left my truck with picked me up from the airport. As soon as we got back to my place—in spite of my feelings for the woman I had just met in Hawaii—we were intimate. The next day, however, out of a desire to be honest with her, I told her about the feelings I had for the woman I met in Hawaii. She didn't take it well. After listening to her cry her heart out and profess her love for me, I decided to take a break from her and the other women I was sexually involved with at the time in order to give the woman from Hawaii my undivided attention.

All was going well, until the day I learned the woman from Hawaii had not been completely honest with me. Upon meeting her, she said she had recently gotten out of a relationship. However, through a mutual acquaintance of ours, I learned she was still involved with a number of men at the time. My heart was broken because I truly had thought she could be the one.

After receiving this disappointing news, I quickly made up with the cheerleader. I soon learned however that she too was still involved in a committed relationship with someone she claimed to be her ex-boyfriend. Feeling betrayed I thought: *And she had the nerve to sit there and profess her love for me after I told her about the woman from Hawaii!* She was not the first cheerleader, nor the last, to lie to me, though. Just before meeting her, I was sexually involved with another cheerleader who I eventually learned was engaged to another man.

I had tried my best to be honest to each woman in my life. Sure, I slept with lots of different women, but when they asked me a question, I was honest, for the most part. But after experiencing so much deception, I arrived at a major crossroad. *Am I going to allow the lies and deception of these three women to have a negative impact on me and begin deceiving and lying as well? Or am I going to come out of all of this with my integrity intact?*

Despite knowing that being deceptive would hurt women—and potentially myself—I swallowed the bitter seed of deception, choosing to also deceive all of the women I became sexually involved with for the remainder of my NFL career. All but one. My mindset switched from "honesty is key" to "I'm going to hurt you before you hurt me." From that day forward, I assumed every woman I met was a liar and could not be trusted. Sadly, I allowed a few hurtful experiences turn into a cycle of deception. I falsely painted all women as deceptive, and went on to hurt many decent women.

I decided to cut off all communication with the three women, removing them from "my rotation"—the women I slept with on a consistent basis. But even with this decision, I still maintained on and off sexual relationships with two out of the three women for the next seven years. And so I found myself involved in many back and forth, up and down, and on and off relationships for the remainder of my career. In the midst of my own lies and deception, I found myself incapable of trusting women. That is, until I met a woman at a music festival in New Orleans.

Leaning over to a buddy standing next to me, I said, "Hey, you see that woman right there? She's going to be my wife!"

"Yeah, right," he said. "And how many times have I heard that before?"

The truth was, he was right. If I had a dollar for every time I had said those words during my collegiate and professional years, I would be the wealthiest man in the world. But this time it was different. With all of my heart I wanted to believe it would be true.

I found her to be well cultured, beautiful, caring, considerate, and highly intelligent. Needless to say, I fell in love with her quickly. We met in July 2002 and I invited her to attend a wedding with me two weeks later. Following the wedding, we parted ways—I headed off to training camp to prepare for the upcoming football season and she headed back down south. I was determined to remain faithful and committed to her. In fact, she would be the only woman during my career—out of a grand total of two committed relationships—that I remained faithful to.

I tried to do everything right with her. For the first time ever, I found it effortless to remain committed to her, even from a distance. I had given her the keys to my heart. The first two months of our relationship went along great, until one night I caught her in a silly lie, which revealed an even greater one—she was involved with someone else. Sure I may have been a tough linebacker in the NFL, but the truth was that I still had the same tender and fragile heart from my childhood. With yet another break in my heart, I decided to once again take back the keys to my heart, refusing to ever give them to another woman. She was the last woman I allowed to get close enough to hurt me. Although we continued an on and off again sexual relationship for the next seven years, I never gave her, or any woman, the full measure of my trust and love. It was just too painful.

After that mess, I went back to simply having fun— intentionally guarding my heart from becoming emotionally attached to any one woman. After learning that eighty-five percent of NFL marriages end in divorce within five years of a player's retirement, I felt good about being single. In fact, after watching some of my teammates go through divorces, I promised myself I would not get married while I played professional ball. I never wanted to experience the pain associated with going through a divorce. Instead, I slept with so many different women that I wouldn't even recognize most of them today. There is one who stands out, however—a woman I met one year after meeting of my ex-girlfriend at the same New Orleans music festival.

In the summer of 2003, a week or so following the music festival, I went back to New Orleans to visit this second woman. After picking me up from the airport, we went straight to the hotel. We entered my hotel room and I dropped my bag on the floor. No more than a few seconds after I took a seat on the bed, she blurted out, "Look, I'm a ni**a wit' mine, so are we gon' fu#@?" Translation: "Let's skip all of the formalities and have intercourse now."

I was completely blown away! With my mouth wide open, I thought, *Whoa! You're in law school and way too beautiful to be talking like that! Besides, that's supposed to be my line!*

Shrugging off the tone of the invitation, I allowed my actions to deliver my response to her question. After this escapade, strangely enough I found myself having a great deal more respect for women who "kept it real" than for women who I assumed were "playing innocent." What I failed to realize, however, is the women that deserved my greatest respect, did not receive it simply because they were not willing to have sex with me on the first night. In other words, I became confused as to who deserved my respect!

For the remainder of my professional football career, I destroyed the innocence of a number of women who were sweet and kind when I first met them, but by the end of our time together were extremely bitter, manipulative, and broken. They became mirror images of the person I had become—a person who resembled Saul of Tarsus.

The Scriptures remind us that Saul spent the majority of his time persecuting and condemning Christians—imprisoning men and women who preached the gospel of Jesus Christ. However, one day he had an encounter with Christ. In the book of Acts, verses 9:20-21, we can see the result of Saul's encounter with Jesus:

> *At once he began to preach in the synagogues that Jesus is the Son of God. All those who heard him were astonished and asked, "Isn't he the man who raised havoc in Jerusalem among those who call on this name? And hasn't he come here to take them as prisoners to the chief priests?" (niv)*

As we see from this passage, Saul's encounter with Jesus changed him. He went from persecuting those who followed Jesus to preaching the gospel of Christ to men and women everywhere! When I played professional football, I was a renegade—better yet a nomadic lion aimlessly wandering alone through the wilderness, consumed with my sexual obsession. Sadly, I also led many women into the same miserable and deserted wilderness—where I used them for my own selfish purposes.

Thank God that, just as Saul's life was changed by his encounter with Jesus, my journey didn't end there.

CHAPTER 6
TRIP AROUND THE WORLD

By February of 2006, I had completed five NFL seasons—a dream come true. That year, I decided to fulfill another one of my childhood dreams with a trip around the world! When I was growing up, I dreamed of traveling to foreign lands, learning from the oldest and wisest people there. Over the course of time, I had become so enthralled by foreign languages that I used to create my own fictitious foreign dialects. Unfortunately, my childhood dream of capturing the perspectives of mankind from different parts of the world became derailed by my obsession with sex.

But now with my childhood dream rekindled, I planned my journey to many exciting places—Fiji, Australia, Indonesia, Singapore, Japan, China, Germany, Egypt, Italy, and Brazil! Before I left, Mr. Sam Jones—who I met during my freshmen year of college and has since become a mentor, a confidant, and one of my closest friends—gave me some much needed traveling tips from his wealth of experience.

"Now, while you're traveling," he said, "if you ever wonder whether or not the food is safe to eat, here are some things you can eat almost anywhere in the world without risking illness. The first food on the list is chocolate, the second is boiled eggs, the third is bread, the next is any vegetables and fruits that have peels, and for a beverage you can always trust bottled water. You'll get your protein from the chocolate, your cholesterol from the boiled eggs, your fiber from the bread, vitamins and nutrients from the fruit and vegetables—and of course water is essential."

I thanked him for his advice and a few days later, with only a shoulder bag to carry my laptop, journal, camera, two t-shirts, flip-flops, and swim trunks, I set out for my adventure!

After leaving United States' soil for the first time in my life, I arrived in Nadi, Fiji around one o'clock in the morning. I checked in at the front desk of my hotel and the attendant politely told me my room would be ready shortly. So I took a seat in the lobby. After all, I was exhausted from having just flown eleven lengthy hours on an airplane! Thirty minutes passed and I still did not have a hotel room. I went back to the front desk and called the attendant over.

I said, "Excuse me, sir, but is there a problem with my reservation?"

"Oh," he responded, "I apologize for the delay. Your room will be ready momentarily."

Taking my seat again, I watched the minutes go by. *There's no need to be impatient. Just relax and give the man a chance to sort it out.* However, after another thirty minutes passed by, I headed back up to the front desk.

"Look, I've been extremely patient but if you can't get me a room right now, I'm going to cancel my reservation and go to another hotel."

"Yes, sir. Your room is ready now, here is your room key. Again, I apologize for the delay. Can I offer you a ride to your room in one of our golf carts?"

"No thank you," I replied—out of frustration—"I'll walk."

So he gave me directions and I headed to my hotel room. Following what turned out to be quite a lengthy walk, I finally arrived at my room. I opened the door and stood surprised. *Are you kidding me!* The room had someone else's belongings scattered all over the place!

After quietly closing the door, I headed back up to the front desk. *I wish I would've let him drive me over here in that stupid cart!* Finally back at the front desk, wiping the sweat from my brow, I said firmly, "Look, I don't know what kind of hotel you guys are running here but I don't have time for this! Someone else's stuff is all over the room. Just cancel the reservation!"

"Oh no!" he responded. "I am so sorry, can you allow me to find you another room?"

"No, thank you!" I said, looking at him as if he were crazy.

Once I received confirmation that my reservation had been cancelled, I was relieved. I had one tiny problem, however—it was a little past two o'clock in the morning and I had no place to sleep! As I stood in the lobby of a hotel in a foreign land, I got on my cell phone and found the phone number to a hotel nearby. When the hotel manager answered I asked, "Hi. Do you have any rooms available right now?"

"No, I'm sorry we do not. However, feel free to try back in the morning!"

Out of desperation, I responded, "I'm sorry, but you don't understand, I really need a room tonight because I have nowhere to sleep! So can you please double check for me?"

"One moment please," he responded, "Ah yes, we do have *one* room available tonight."

"Okay," I responded out of relief, "I'll take it!"

"Well, just so you know the rate is—"

"It's okay," I interrupted. "I'll be there in five minutes. I don't care what the rate is!"

Moments later, following my arrival, I checked in at the front desk. After extending the reservation to my entire stay in Fiji, I handed him payment and breathed a big sigh of relief. After traveling eleven hours on a plane and spending over two hours trying to find an *unoccupied* room to sleep in, I finally walked into my room, dropped my shoulder bag to the floor and, without showering or even removing my clothing, I collapsed into the bed.

Waking very early the next morning, I looked out of my window in awe and amazement at the beauty before my eyes—lush green trees, dark brown soil, colorful flowers covering the ground, and the scent of dew. After finally getting settled in, I became "Ian the Explorer."

I roamed around the beach and the hotel grounds, learning the hotel had only been open for a few months. There were not many guests, naturally causing me to question the integrity of the hotel manager. *Did they lie to me about having only the Presidential Suite available for the remainder of the week?* I wondered. But I was not about to let my thoughts of being taken advantage of bother me! After exploring a bit, I decided to take a seat poolside. Although I had seen a number of beautifully sculpted hotel pools in the States, this pool took the prize! Beautifully decorated with native flowers, the pool stretched nearly the entire length of the hotel and was just steps away from the ocean shore. After spending the entire day in and out of the pool, I decided to grab a bite to eat and call it a day.

Rising quite early the next morning, hungry and refreshed, I needed food! Recalling the advice of Mr. Jones, I ate bread, a chocolate bar, fresh fruit, and washed it all down with a bottle of water. Following breakfast, I headed back to the pool.

While sitting poolside, during a brief pause from writing in my journal, a group of beautiful women walked out towards the pool. *You've got to be kidding me!* I thought. Turns out the women were professional models from Australia and New Zealand who were there for a photo shoot for the hotel's brochure. Quickly switching into "chase" mode, it didn't take me long to hook up with one of them. As we spent time together one afternoon, we mutually agreed to keep our interaction casual, not allowing our emotions to get involved.

The following day, I met up with her and her co-workers, which included a woman who happened to be far more beautiful than the first woman I met. Out of sheer greed and selfishness, I thought, *I'll try to get them both.* Following breakfast and spending the day with the first woman I met, later that evening, I began my pursuit of the second woman. However, once the first woman became aware of my efforts to pursue her younger, more attractive co-worker, she successfully convinced her not to spend any time with me. *Oh well, I'm headed to Australia in the morning, so who cares!*

After getting settled into the Gold Coast—a beach town located on the East Coast of the Australian Continent—I decided to take a stroll through a local mall on the pier. While leisurely walking past a store, I noticed a beautiful woman standing in a women's clothing store. After making a comical excuse for entering the store, I extended an invitation for her to join me for dinner, which she accepted. I enjoyed the dinner with her—good conversation and food—as we dined out on the pier under the moonlit sky. After dinner she accompanied me back to my hotel room. We spent time talking and getting to know one another a bit more. After learning she was from New Zealand and discovering a few other minor details about her, she left without even a kiss.

The next morning I ventured out to explore one of Australia's most popular beach towns. During my visit to a local zoo, I got to see kangaroos for the first time in my life! Seeing kangaroos quickly became one of the highlights of my visit to the land Down Under. I also had the pleasure of holding a Koala bear, which freaked me out a little bit because its razor sharp claws pierced tiny holes in my shirt.

With my tour of the zoo complete, I made my way to the beach where I witnessed what I call "The Australian Machine"—Australia's world-class swimmers and lifeguards—at work. While walking the beach, I also observed the next generation of "The Australian Machine" perform routine training exercises. *These kids train as hard as I do!* I thought, as I watched them participate in sprinting drills across the beach to the shoreline.

After walking the beach, I headed back to the hotel to meet up with my new "Kiwi" friend. We met up at my hotel, where she told me there was a special place she wanted to take me. I told her to lead the way. She took me to a place called Burleigh Heads—a small area located just South of the Gold Coast—where we walked up to an observatory. Reaching the highest point in the observatory, I learned why this was one of her favorite places to visit. We had an amazing panoramic view of the entire coastline. The view was breathtaking! After spending an hour or so walking and talking our way through the observatory, we watched surfers flirt with death—surfing near large black boulders near the shoreline. A young schoolgirl, accompanied by a group of her classmates, began shouting, "Catch it, catch it, CATCH IT!" as she pointed to the sea.

Growing up surrounded by lakes—not the ocean—I had absolutely no idea what she was talking about. But I turned back to the sea for a second look, and it didn't take long to realize what she was saying—*she's telling the surfers to catch the wave!* Finally figuring out what her excitement was all about, I began laughing out loud, gaining a whole new understanding of the phrase "catch it."

After spending most of the afternoon in Burleigh Heads, we decided to grab a bite to eat. Walking back to the hotel after dinner, the rain began pouring down. Taking cover under a bus awning, we caught each other's eyes. Like a scene out of a movie, we kissed—the type of dramatic kiss you see just before the final credits begin to roll—as raindrops softly applauded.

We headed back to the hotel where, much to my surprise, she declined my invitation to stay the night. When she turned to leave, I realized that unlike so many of the women I had become accustomed to hooking up with—there were women in the world with values and standards. After parting ways that evening, I did not see her again for the remainder of my stay on the Gold Coast. Needless to say, I would soon forget about her after landing in The Republic of Singapore.

I arrived in Singapore extremely disappointed. I had already visited two amazing countries—and still had not had sex. Immediately, I set out on the prowl. I went to a local bar and while seated alone at a table, I noticed a beautiful Asian woman accompanied by two other women. After purchasing them a round of drinks, they immediately came over and joined me. Communicating with them was a bit of a challenge because they were Vietnamese. So, after asking them a few questions, one of them said, "We are working." *Okay,* I thought. *Good for you!* When she recognized that I did not fully understand what she was saying, she repeated her statement—but this time with more emphasis.

"No, we are WORKING!"

Then a light switch came on. *Oh, they are prostitutes!*

After learning their profession, and having never had sex with three women at the same time up to this point, I immediately asked them if they were interested in coming with me back to my hotel room and they all agreed. Being in a foreign country and having no knowledge of the laws—or really who these women were—I took a little precaution. Before allowing them to enter my hotel room I asked, "Are you police officers?"

"No, man," responded the leader of the group in her broken English. "We no police."

"Okay. Open your purses so I can make sure you don't have any weapons."

While looking at me strangely, the leader spoke to the other two in their native tongue.

"Ah yes, okay," they replied.

After finding no weapons and realizing how silly I looked and sounded, I finally invited them in to my room. Once they came into my room they wasted little time doing what I hired them to do. And after having sex with them all, they left.

As the door clicked shut, I sat in silence.

I began to realize how much of a pig I had become and overwhelming feelings of conviction rushed over me, just as they had many times before. Sadly, once I fell asleep and woke up the next morning, those feelings were nowhere to be found. I spent the rest of my time in Singapore exploring and shopping—alone. As I boarded the plane for Indonesia, thoughts of my inexcusable actions and behavior sobered me up once again.

During my first night in Bali, I witnessed something I had never seen before. After settling into my hotel, I hired a driver to take me out on the town. Once I realized the nightclubs didn't open until around one or two in the morning, I reluctantly took the driver's advice and went to a karaoke bar. I thought, *Why does he keep asking, "I take you to karaoke now?" I mean what the heck is so exciting about a karaoke bar?* The answer was soon made clear.

My first suspicion that this was no ordinary karaoke bar occurred as we pulled up. Men with machine guns searched our vehicle. After their dogs sniffed and searched around the vehicle, the driver was allowed to pull into the parking lot and I exited the vehicle. Not really sure what I was getting into, I entered the red building ahead of me.

Once inside, my understanding didn't get any clearer. The interior walls were painted the same color red as the exterior, and on a stage was an Asian woman dressed in a pink and red dress singing her rendition of what sounded like a dying cat. *What the heck did he bring me here for?* After standing there for a brief moment, a man approached me.

"Follow me."

Out of sheer curiosity I did what I was told. I followed the short man down a long hallway. As we turned a corner my mouth opened wide. I could not believe what I was seeing—behind a glass wall was a room full of women with numbers taped to their shirts, seated in stadium-style bleachers. *I'm in a brothel!* I noticed some of the women using the glass wall as a mirror to fix their makeup. As I stood in shock, an older Asian woman came up to me and said, "Which number you choose?"

Scanning through the room full of Asian women, I hesitated for a moment. *Is this really happening? This is so wrong. Am I really about to pick a number?* Then one of the women caught my eye.

"Number *@."

"Okay. You no take her to hotel, you stay here."

"No," I replied, "I want to go back to my hotel." I thought, *It'd be just my luck for this place to get raided by the police while I'm here!*

"Okay," she responded, "then you choose #@, #@, #@, or #@."

When I chose a different number, she said, "Okay, you pay me now."

Handing her a fist full of money, I quickly walked out of the karaoke bar with the woman I chose and headed back to my hotel. I tipped the driver handsomely and expressed my gratitude to him for taking me to "karaoke," then anxiously headed to my bungalow. The door had barely clicked shut when we started to go at it. Suddenly, for some reason, I stopped and moved to the edge of the bed.

"I can't do this," I said. "We're not having sex. You can leave."

I handed her money to pay for a cab and she left. After she left, thoughts began flooding my mind. *Why am I so sex crazed? Why am I paying for sex, let alone picking up women from brothels in foreign countries where I don't even know the consequences for getting caught?*

I began thinking of all the women back in the States and how, although enjoying the time spent with them, none of them satisfied my insatiable desire. Sitting on the edge of the bed, I wondered if one woman was ever going to be enough to satisfy me. Perhaps this was another reason I preferred being intimate with women with whom I had no emotional ties. It kept my heart safe.

My heart may have been safe, but my physical safety was another matter altogether.

The next day, while enviously watching two women dive into the Indian Ocean and another local surfer catch wave after wave, I naively thought, *That looks like so much fun! If they can do it, I can do it!* With this thought fresh in my mind, I left the comfort of my cushioned seat and walked out to the shoreline.

Not being too familiar with the ocean, I took a few mental notes on what technique to use from the two women down the shore. With my newly acquired knowledge, I walked confidently into the sea. As the first wave roared against the shore, I managed to dive underneath it, just as I had seen the women do. After resurfacing, the water level had gone from my knees to my chest.

So far, so good, I thought.

Then, while standing completely still, the most powerful undercurrent I have ever felt swept me clear off of my feet!

I panicked!

While frantically trying to swim toward the shore, I regained my footing on the ocean floor and ran as fast as I could onto dry land! Reaching the safety of solid ground, I caught myself looking around to see if anyone had witnessed my panic attack. Out of breath and sitting on the beach, I began laughing out loud.

Looking back, it seems that being caught in that undertow was exactly what was happening in the rest of my life.

Looking out at the ocean's surface, I was captivated and lured in by its mystique. Carelessly diving into the sea, I never stopped to weigh or consider the risk. In spite of being refreshed and cooled, the strength and power of the ocean nearly cost me my life.

Similarly, my obsession with beautiful women lured me into a lifestyle dominated with evening after evening of nightclubs and strip clubs. As I dove carelessly into having sex with multiple women, I was unaware, or perhaps in denial, of the consequences of my actions—consequences that could have easily destroyed me. After surviving the undercurrent of Bali, I was off to Japan.

During my first day in Tokyo, I walked through the Ginza shopping district and looked nearly one hour for an ATM machine that accepted my bankcard. After finally getting some cash, I did a little shopping. Stepping into a shoe store, I literally spent ten minutes trying to ask the shoe salesmen if they had a size thirteen. I finally asked them to give me paper and pen. After writing the number "13" on the piece of paper and handing it to them, they quickly looked at each other and began laughing out loud.

"Oh no, no. So sorry." Joining them in laughter, they talked to one another in Japanese, probably saying, *"Crazy American! Nobody in Japan wears a size thirteen!"* Needless to say, that was my last stop in a shoe store during my time in Japan!

Tokyo was also the place where I enjoyed the best seafood ever, thanks to a recommendation from the concierge at my hotel—the only English-speaking person I met in Tokyo. A taxi took me from my hotel to one of the best steakhouses in the city. Seated alongside strangers, in front of a large tabletop-cooking surface, the chef pulled out live prawns, sizzling them right in front of us. One woman had to turn away because she couldn't stand to watch the prawns squirm as they cooked.

After the chef sliced and dished the prawns to customers, he scraped together the last few scraps—the heads and tails of the prawns—offering me one of the heads. I politely declined. *There's no way I'm eating that!* I thought.

Moments later, hoping for better luck, he offered me one of the tails. Considering this a better option at the time—and perhaps feeling the need to prove my fearlessness—I ate it.

"Ah, you no eat the head, but you eat the butt!"

We both laughed hysterically. In fact, for the remainder of the meal, every time we made eye contact we shared a friendly smile.

My original plan was to visit Beijing, China after spending time in Tokyo. But, because I failed to obtain the proper visa, I was stranded at the airport ticket counter in Tokyo. My impetuous nature kicked in. Not wanting to spend the extra day in Tokyo waiting for the visa, I decided to take a little detour! I asked the customer service representative to send me to any country west of Japan that did not require me to obtain a visa.

"Okay, sir, I can get you on a flight to Hong Kong if you would like."

"Sure," I replied, "why not?"

With my flight boarding only minutes after I made it through security, I phoned my mother—*thank God for my mom*—and asked her to cancel my hotel reservation in Beijing and book me a new hotel reservation in Hong Kong. My mother, of course, had a million questions.

"Why aren't you going to Beijing? When are you arriving in Hong Kong? How am I going to make the reservation? What do you want me to do again?"

I didn't have much time, however, so I had to keep our conversation short. After finally giving my mother only the details she needed, I set out for Hong Kong—where I would have a once in a lifetime experience.

During my second day in Hong Kong I met a group of people in the hotel lounge—two married couples from Australia, and an older gentleman from the States who turned out to be the former owner of an NFL franchise. Go figure. Since they seemed to know the lay of the land, I decided to tag along with them.

On our first night out together, they took me to Lang Kwai Fong—the Bourbon Street of Hong Kong. After being encouraged by the wives not to chase women because of the high number of sex change operations in that part of the world, I decided it best to leave the bar district. I headed to another location with the older gentlemen and one of his Asian friends who had to be at least seventy years old. To my surprise they took me to a brothel.

Not being interested in any of the women I saw, I wound up back in my hotel room alone, thinking, *I definitely don't want to end up like these old guys! I mean they're seventy plus years old and married—and they hunt and chase women more than I do!* In fact, the very next night, the guy from the States jumped out of a moving car in his effort to chase after a couple of women. He ended up taking them back to the hotel. *Dude, you could have killed yourself!* I thought, shaking my head.

I should have been the last person on the face of the earth judging or criticizing him—or anyone else for that matter— during that period of my life. At the time, I simply could not understand why a man his age seemed to be even more determined to chase after women than I was. Looking back, I now see a strange irony in how I felt. It was as if I was beginning to get a true glimpse at who I was becoming, as my life at the time, was "all about the chase".

The day before I left Hong Kong, oddly enough, I had a random conversation with one of the husbands about the exotic dancer from Tampa. I don't know why she popped into my head, but she did. After shrugging my thoughts of her off, I decided to hang out in the party district with my new acquaintances. We bar hopped all night. Then, while standing in the middle of the street in Lang Kwai Fong one of the wives said, as she pointed over my shoulder with a frightened look on her face,

"Ian, I think there's someone running up to you."

Turning around, the dancer I'd just spoke about leaped into my arms! *Am I dreaming?* As we embraced and greeted one another, the husband I had mentioned her to whispered, "Hey Mate, is that the same woman you were talking about earlier?"

"Yep," I said, still amazed. "Absolutely unbelievable!"

"Wow!"

As we began to get caught up, it became quite clear that she was not completely sober. Although I wanted to spend time with her, years prior I had made a decision to never allow myself to be intimate with women who were high or intoxicated—so we parted ways.

As I walked away from this amazing encounter, I began to think about God's ability to work in mysterious ways. It would be years before God finally revealed to me why He allowed this unexpected encounter, as well as others like it, to occur. What I didn't realize at that moment, though, was that the night still held more in store for me. It began earlier that day when one of the wives made a subtle comment while we were all sitting in the lounge of the hotel.

"You know," she said, "before I married my husband I used to love dating black men." I had pretended not to hear this. But following the departure of my friend, both of the women's husbands disappeared soon after the couples and I went to another bar. Noticing the time was getting late, and remembering I had an early flight to catch, I decided to call it a night. As I walked out of the bar, the wife who made the comment about dating black men followed me to the taxi.

"You should stay here with me."

"Where is your husband?" I asked with a chuckle.

"I don't know!" she replied, "Probably out screwing some Asian chick! Why don't we hang out?"

Declining her offer as politely as I could, she shared with me that she and her husband had an "understanding"—as long as they didn't know what the other was doing, they could do whatever they wanted. I tried to tell her I wasn't interested and started to get into the car, then, she tried to grab my arm. I pulled away and instructed the driver to take me to the hotel. Although this was not the first time I had been propositioned by a married woman, I felt somewhat saddened by her desperation.

Sitting in the back of the taxi, driving through the streets of Hong Kong, I thought: *Who are you to judge her? Take a look in the mirror.*

The next morning I boarded a plane to Frankfurt, Germany.

CHAPTER 7
SEX AROUND THE WORLD AND BACK

I arrived in Germany only to realize it was the middle of winter. And as I stood outside of the airport in Frankfurt, with only a thin fleece to shield me from the freezing wind, thoughts of finding a pretty European woman to warm me up began to flood my mind. Having studied the German language for a combined eight years in both, high school and college, I always dreamed of visiting Deutschland. So after getting into a cab, I wasted no time testing my Deutsch on the cab driver, who complimented me in English, "You speak good German." I guess all of my German classes paid off after all!

After the driver dropped me off at my hotel, I needed something to eat, and thankfully the quaint hotel had a small restaurant connected to it. I sat in amazement as my waiter took my order in both English and German, and then spoke Punjabi to one of his co-workers. Refreshed by the hot meal, I got into a cab to go to the Red Light District. I was dropped off right in the center of the district, and I set out to hunt.

The first building I walked into reminded me of a haunted house. There were no lights and in the center of the lobby stood an oddly shaped booth with dark tinted windows. Having no idea what to do or where to go, I walked cautiously around a corner and up a flight of stairs. Part way down a long hall, I looked into an open door and saw a half-naked woman sitting on a bed. I couldn't believe it—*This entire apartment building is full of prostitutes.* As I continued down the hall, half-naked women came out of their rooms and stood in their doorways saying, "*Kommen Sie, bitte*" (which means "Come here, please"). I entered one of the rooms, and after hearing the list of services the woman there provided, the clock started for my half-hour of pleasure.

As the clock sped on, the woman took her time until, before I knew it, my thirty minutes had expired. She abruptly stopped and said, "Your time is up. Do you want to pay for more time?"

"Are you kidding me? No!"

Irritated and annoyed at her business-like nature, I walked down the street to a nearby strip club I noticed just before entering the brothel. Frustrated with the time and money I had just wasted, I took a seat. Quickly catching the eye of an attractive woman, I asked her to leave work early and come with me to my hotel. And for the right price, she did. The moment we got back to my hotel room, I let out my sexual frustrations, paid her, and then she left.

Sitting in the silence of my hotel room, the familiar questions began to surface in my mind. *What is wrong with me? Why can't I go without having sex?* As I sought for answers, one thing I knew for sure—God had witnessed my sexually immoral behavior and was not pleased. As I lay in bed that night, on the edge of falling asleep, my questions and concerns faded away.

The next morning I boarded a flight to Cairo, Egypt, but when I got there, I experienced my second panic attack of the trip. While walking with one of the hotel greeters to customs, he politely asked me to give him my passport. He explained that he could get my visa for me and get me through the customs line faster. Despite being unsure whether or not I should trust him, I reluctantly handed him my passport anyway.

As I stood alone watching him inch closer and closer to the front of the line I began thinking, *How do I know if he really works for the hotel? He could be lying to me.* The more I thought about the possibility, the more paranoid I became. Out of concern, I yelled out his name.

He did not turn around.

Maybe he didn't hear me, I thought. So I yelled his name again and again, but still no response. Finally, as he neared the front of the line, out of sheer panic I walked up to him and grabbed his arm firmly.

"Hey, you didn't hear me calling you? Give me my passport!"

His face became flushed and, quickly handing me my passport, he nervously responded, "I am sorry, Sir, but I did not hear you."

After explaining my concern to him, he walked me over to a group of his co-workers who confirmed his employment with the hotel. Being confident he was who he said he was, I handed him my passport again.

While awaiting his return, I couldn't help but notice the aged wooden podiums and the frustrated look on the faces of the over-worked customs agents. As my eyes journeyed around the outdated airport, I met eyes with an Egyptian man who observed my panic attack.

"You can never be too careful, my friend," he remarked. I thanked him for his remark and we both smiled.

Minutes later, the hotel greeter returned with my passport and visa and escorted me around the lengthy customs lines to the entrance of the airport, which was packed with hundreds of people waiting for their loved ones to arrive. The faces of the Egyptian people looked much different than what I had envisioned when I first heard Mr. Pipkin, my sixth grade homeroom teacher, talk about his trips to Egypt. Expecting Egyptians to look a lot more like me, I stood both corrected and a bit culture shocked to learn that Egyptian people resemble light-skinned Middle Easterners—more so than the dark-skinned tribal Africans I grew up seeing in magazines and watching on television.

Reaching the entrance to the airport, the hotel greeter escorted me to my driver's vehicle, which was in the process of receiving a parking ticket for being in a no parking zone. Getting into the backseat of the vehicle, I noticed that instead of a gun, the officer carried a fifteen-inch machete blade. *I wonder if he's ever had to use it?* The driver reluctantly received his ticket and we sped off for the hotel.

I quickly settled into my hotel room and then walked up to the rooftop pool, surveying the gorgeous, panoramic view of the Nile River and the pyramids. Having heard about this ancient land my whole life, I wanted to take a mental picture of everything I saw—from the golden sun setting over the Sahara Desert, to the tourist and fishing boats that lined the banks of the river.

Later that evening, I decided to have dinner at a restaurant next door to the hotel. The host seated me next to a table with three beautiful Egyptian women and I transitioned into chase mode, thinking, *I'll pay for their dinner!* I summoned my waiter and asked him to bring me their bill.

"I am sorry, sir, but I cannot allow you to pay for their dinner."

"Okay," I said, arrogantly, "can I speak to the manager?" Moments later, the manager arrived at my table.

"Hello, sir, how may I help you?"

"Yeah, I would like to pay for their dinner." I responded, motioning to the table with the three beautiful women, "Could you please bring me their bill?"

"Um, sir," he said politely, "do you know them?"

"Uh, no!" I said peevishly. "I just want to pay for their dinner!"

"Okay, sir. Let me go ask the ladies if they will allow you to pay for their dinner."

"Fine!"

He walked over to their table and spoke to the ladies in Arabic as he poured water into their glasses. When he returned, he said, "I am very sorry, but they have declined your offer."

What?!? I thought. *What a liar!*

Truth is, my pride and ego had taken a huge blow. Out of frustration—and embarrassment—I paid for my meal and arrogantly walked out of the restaurant without even taking my dinner! Although I was frustrated and upset, I came to realize that Egyptian men would not stand for Egyptian women being devalued and treated like objects. I had no choice but to simply let go of my frustration. They reacted the same way I would have if some arrogant jerk tried to purchase the attention of my daughter, mother or sisters. Needless to say, after getting over my bruised ego, I developed a new respect for Egyptian men.

The next morning, I got up bright and early to meet a woman who worked at the concierge. She had asked me to breakfast the day before and I of course couldn't say no. She had the look of an Egyptian Princess—golden skin and beautiful, long black hair. She made the classic uniform she wore look as if it had been custom made to fit her sculpted figure. While sorting through the food choices she urged me to try some of the Egyptian cuisine. Fearing the worst, however, I stuck to my bread, chocolate, fruit and water.

We had a pleasant conversation. She shared with me that Egyptians with light skin complexion are awarded better paying jobs than Egyptians with a dark skinned complexion. I also learned that careers in hotel hospitality are highly coveted. I was enlightened and intrigued. I asked if she would be interested in having dinner with me. She told me she would check her schedule and let me know later—I was optimistic.

Following breakfast, I made arrangements to take a tour of the Cairo Museum and the Pyramids with one of the young men from the concierge who volunteered to be my tour guide. As I wandered from room to room, I found the museum to be extremely educational. However, after an hour or so of looking at ancient mummies and ancient artifacts, without being allowed to take photographs, I decided to head to the Pyramids and the Sphinx.

In spite of the unexpected entrance fee to gain access to the pyramids, I enjoyed touring the enormous wonders. I took tons of photographs—officers on camels, school kids running and laughing—all with the giant structures and the Sahara Desert in the background. I was so enthralled by the pyramids, I found myself losing track of time as I listened to my tour guide. While walking from the pyramids to the Sphinx, an Egyptian man, accompanied by his friends, shouted a remark at us in Arabic. And when my tour guide shouted back and began laughing, I asked, "What did he say?"

"He was talking trash because he knows you are an American," he replied.

"So what did you say to him?"

"I told him you were a professional boxer and he'd better shut up!" We both laughed.

Following my tour of the ancient Egyptian ruins, I called the woman from the concierge to see if we had a date for dinner—only to find that she had to help her cousin prepare for a wedding party, so she said. I actually thought she discerned my dishonorable intentions and declined. So without a date for the evening, I ordered room service and watched a movie. Now this made her the second woman I had come across on my trip that displayed moral values and standards that she managed to uphold. Sitting in my room, enjoying room service, I thought, *I profess to be a follower of Jesus Christ—but what standards do I live by?* While this thought stayed with me for the next few days, it would take a few more years to properly assess and address my lack of moral standards and values. But I couldn't think too much about that now—my next stop was Rome, Italy!

The moment I arrived at my hotel in Rome, I asked the concierge to recommend a restaurant where I could enjoy some authentic Italian cuisine—and it was just my luck that one of the best restaurants in all of Rome happened to be located directly across the square from my hotel.

After being seated, for some strange reason I suddenly felt rushed. *What are you rushing for? It's not like you're on a tight schedule,* I thought. Sadly, we Americans are so accustomed to rushing in and out of restaurants. I decided to slow down—enough so that I could actually taste the food. While moving at a snail's pace through my dinner, I noticed two beautiful Italian women take a seat at a table across the room. Then, the unexpected happened—one of the women got up and walked towards me. *Is she walking over here?* I wondered. She approached me with unprecedented boldness and confidence, then following our introduction, I offered her a seat. We talked briefly and I invited her and her friend to join me for dinner—and an excellent dinner it was! The amazing pasta, company, and ambience—all made me think, *so this is what the Romans do!*

Following dinner, I thanked the women for their company and called it a night. Although we saw each other again, there were no sparks—I simply enjoyed their company. As I lay in bed that night, I took stock of all I had experienced on my trip thus far. I had seen women treated as objects of lust in Indonesia, and I had seen the honor of women defended in Egypt. I, however, was trapped somewhere in the middle—still questioning my lack of moral values and standards.

The alarm clock went off early the next morning and after a quick breakfast, it was off to see the city! I walked and walked and then walked some more—until I could not walk anymore. I toured the ancient Coliseum, the Piazza di Spagna (the Spanish Steps), the Piazza Venezia, and many of the other historical sites located throughout the ancient city of Rome. I found the Italian people to be charming and quickly found myself falling in love with them and their culture—as the Italians possess a near perfect blend of style, confidence, and humility. Finally, after days of touring myself out of my shoes and eating myself into a pair of larger sized jeans, I boarded a plane to my last destination, Rio de Janeiro, Brazil!

But first I had a layover in Lisbon, Spain where a beautiful Brazilian woman caught my eye. *Should I go talk to her? Nah, hopefully she'll get on the same flight as me.* The boarding process finally began and she headed toward the boarding area. *Sweet!* Although the chances of her sitting next to me on the plane were slim to none, I thought, *I've never been lucky enough to have a beautiful woman sit next to me on an airplane, but I have a feeling that this just might be my lucky day.*

After boarding, much to my surprise, she sat in a seat directly across the aisle from me. *Close enough!* I stored my bag and took a trip to the restroom and upon my return she had moved to the seat right next to me! *Huh?* It just so happened that an elderly couple had asked if she would switch seats with one of them so they could sit together. Shortly after take off, I introduced myself only to face a huge language barrier—she didn't speak English and I didn't speak Portuguese. We were in for a long flight!

For the next nine hours straight, neither of us slept a wink, as we tried our best to communicate—using in-flight magazines, photos, pen and paper, and all of our senses. During the course of the flight, we experienced every non-verbal emotion one could imagine. We were both extremely frustrated by the language barrier. We laughed and shared looks of which only our actions could express, we shared a few kisses and at one point she even shed a few tears—why I will never know.

By the end of the flight, despite not being able to understand one word she said, I had it all worked out! She agreed to come stay with me at my hotel for a few days before returning to her home in Florianopolis—a small island off the coast of Brazil.

We exited together as if we had been traveling with each other all along. My hormones raced as I thought of the adventure that awaited me! Little did I know, however, that watching her walk through customs would be the last time I would ever see her. Sadly, no one informed me in Lisbon that I needed to purchase a visa to enter the country of Brazil. After being detained by customs agents for an hour or so, the pronouncement came:

"Sir, you are going back to Lisbon!"

"No, I'm not!" I firmly replied, "Send me home to the US—because that's where my next flight is headed. Here's my ticket."

I handed the agent my ticket to Miami and they booked me on a flight to Washington, DC later that evening. As I sat in the airport waiting for my flight, I looked out at the beautiful countryside. *There's got to be a pretty good reason why God's not allowing me to spend any time in Rio . . .*

Arriving back in the States, I felt extremely disappointed in myself. Having left the US with aspirations of seeing the world, I returned having utilized most of my time and energy chasing women. My thoughts immediately went to the women who were disappointed with me for not taking them with me. As it turned out, although I left the women behind—I didn't leave my obsession with sex. And soon after getting reacquainted with my usual surroundings and stable of women, I began preparing for what would prove to be my second to last NFL season.

Sitting at my locker one day, I received an odd phone call from my older cousin Darrian. Throughout the course of my entire NFL career, and in spite of myself at times, he and I had consistent conversations about God, and this particular conversation was no different. He shared with me details from a prophetic dream that one of his friends had about me. He asked me if I had recently thought about retiring, and although I told him no, I truly had no idea what God had in store for my near or distant future. Ending our conversation, it would not be for another several years that we would realize the meaning and purpose of his friend's dream. Below is a small portion of the dream he would eventually share with me, in its entirety, in the spring of 2010:

> *I shared with Darrian that I felt like Ian would soon be stepping away from the NFL to pursue ministry. I also stated I believed Ian had a call upon his life and I reflected upon the legacy and mantle of ministry within Darrian's family.*

Had I read the email back in 2006, I probably would have immediately dismissed it. I've heard my fair share of bizarre remarks and questions over the years. In fact, during this period of my life I believed very little of what anyone said to me. Whether it was one of my coaches congratulating me on having a good game, a woman professing her love to me, or a total stranger telling me how great a person I was—I didn't believe a word of it. I just figured people were saying what they did because of some ulterior motive. Looking back, I don't think people believed much of what they said either.

One day while walking out onto the practice field in Tampa, one of my teammates remarked, "Ha! I already know how I'm gon' die—by getting shot, or catching AIDS!"

"Dude, you're an idiot!" I responded out of shock, "Listen to yourself! Did you just hear what you just said?"

I judged him because I didn't want to acknowledge the truth—that my own senseless choices and decisions could very well cause me to end up dying in the same manner. While carelessly having unprotected sex with countless women, or while hanging out at a nightclub, I could have easily contracted AIDS. Some random person with absolutely no regard for life could have shot and killed me. Thinking about the possibility of a sudden and unexpected death reminds me of an incident I'll never forget involving one of my former teammates—Darrent Williams.

On the Friday before the last game of the 2006 season, I arrived at the Broncos practice facility a little earlier than usual. Oddly enough, on this particular morning I felt like God told me to place a few gospel music CD's in the locker room stereo, which had never been done in my seven years with the Broncos. While sitting quietly in my locker, one of my teammates walked in and we greeted one another in our usual way—with a BIG smile! It didn't matter where we were—on the practice field, hanging out with friends, or on an airplane headed to play our next opponent—we always greeted each other with a huge smile.

He walked to his locker and began preparing himself for another day's work, when he looked over at me and asked, "Ian, you put this CD in, didn't you?"

"Yep!" I replied.

After a few more moments of silence, to my surprise he began singing one of the songs. Shocked, I asked, "Man, what you know about this?"

"Oh, my mama used to play this when I was growing up whenever it was time to clean up."

"My mama did too!" I said, laughing.

Then we sat silently at our lockers simply enjoying the company of "peace" and "quiet"—before they were brutally forced out by "loudness" which always came charging its way into the locker room with the rest of my teammates.

As I observed him for a moment, it seemed as though the words of the song took him to a place of deep thought. In that moment, I remember lying back in my locker, covering my eyes with a sweatshirt and saying a silent prayer for him, *Lord, let the words of this song minister to him.*

On Sunday, the game came and went, and honestly I don't remember who won or lost. Following the game, each of us had our own plans for bringing in the New Year, so we all went our separate ways.

I decided to go meet up with my girlfriend at a jazz club in downtown Denver. After bringing in the New Year with her, I went straight home. It was around two or three o'clock in the morning when my brother, Jeremy, came rushing into my bedroom. He was breathing heavily.

"Ian, Mom just woke me up and told me to make sure you were home. She's watching the news and said one of your teammates was shot and killed!"

"Huh?" I responded, lifting my head up from my pillow. "What did you say?"

He repeated the news again. I put my head back down on my pillow for a moment in total disbelief.

I just saw him full of life, running up and down a football field!

Still in total disbelief, I got out of bed and went to find my mother. I found her sitting in front of the television, tears slowly streaming down her face. I sat down next to her, grabbing her hand, and listened to the news report. It was true—"D-Will" had been shot and killed in a drive-by shooting moments after his limousine drove away from a nightclub.

While holding back tears, I looked over at my mother. Turning back toward the screen, I began to weep—my heart ached.

"Mom, I feel so guilty," I sobbed, "I should have done more, or said more. All of the times I sat and played chess and cards with him in the locker room or on the airplane, were opportunities I could've used to talk to him about Jesus—but now he's gone."

When my tears finally stopped, I immediately thought of sitting in the locker room a few days prior, listening to gospel music. You see, "D-Will" was the teammate who laughed with me about our mother's "clean up music."

I shared with my mother how I prayed and asked God to minister to him through the words of the song. She tried her best to comfort me. "Ian, God instructed you to play that music so he could listen to it. Stop looking at everything you didn't do and be thankful for being obedient in doing what God instructed you to do."

After hearing her words, "peace" comforted me—as my mother and I said a prayer for his family and loved ones.

When I think of my teammate's tragic and senseless death, I think of the times I too could have fallen victim—from the time a guy jumped out of a car and pulled a gun on my friends and me, only for it to jam when he pulled the trigger, to the night I narrowly escaped death in a bar as a man frantically reached for the gun he had buried in his left pocket. Or the time I entered a woman's hotel room, only to be greeted by her angry boyfriend. In all of my brushes with death, I have learned that dangerous people look to start trouble, while most victims never see trouble until it's too late. Unfortunately, at the time, I often found myself in harm's way because I was carelessly consumed by my own lust.

As my teammates and I joked one day, laughing and sharing various accounts of the different experiences we had with women—I remember one guy saying, "Sh#*, I'll hit [have sex with] the wind if it stands still!"

As I thought about his words, even if only for a split second, I realized how careless we were being with our body, minds, and souls. The countless number of outlandish remarks and filthy comments I said and heard had become so ridiculous, I began losing any sense of what was truth and what were lies. It became difficult for me to separate fact from fiction as I began to resemble the type of men I used to despise and judge—men who treated women as disposable objects and simply used them for sex.

CHAPTER 8
MY SURRENDER

In the years leading up to my surrender, with all the "juggling" I was doing in my dating and sex life, I was nothing more than a clown in the circus. But over time, I found it extremely difficult to spend enough quality time with women to keep them happy. So, in addition to giving each woman a predetermined measure of my time and affection, showering them with gifts seemed to keep them satisfied and content during my absence. Throughout the course of my NFL career I wasted hundreds of thousands of dollars on women—vehicles, jewelry, furniture, kitchen appliances, college tuition, paying off student loans, even helping a few women purchase their first homes—all for the sake of keeping them happy. I even paid for the funeral of a woman's family member. The price of being involved with more than one woman at a time was not cheap!

One Christmas, I purchased three identical watches, thinking: *None of them know each other so they'll never find out.* Thinking back now, I should have invested in a car service—

since I frequently hired drivers to transport women in whichever city, state, or country I was in at the time.

Meeting women and splurging on them became a way of life for me. While out one night in Denver, I met a woman who attended one of the local colleges. After inviting her to one of my games, I sent a limousine to pick her and a group of her friends up from Boulder. *Sending a limo to pick up her and her friends will make her want to have sex,* I thought. Unfortunately, I was right. A few days later we began a sexual relationship that spanned over a four-year period. In another example of my ability to waste money, after giving a woman a car when I ended our sexual relationship, she sold it. After seeing her in a different car one day, I asked, "So what happened to the car I gave you?"

"It reminded me of you," she admitted, "so I had to get rid of it."

Wow, I thought, *hope she got a good deal.*

Did I have to spend money to sleep with women? Not at all. However, while strolling in and out of designer clothing stores and boutiques, I took pleasure in observing the childlike expression that danced on each of their faces, when I said, "Get whatever you want!"

Some women even became angry after I refused to give them certain items I had purchased for them during the course of our involvement—I guess they felt as if I was indebted to them for the time we were involved. When recognizing how anxious and desperate they were—over a snowboard, or an article of clothing—I eventually gave in to them, as it became clear that they cared more about the items I purchased for them, than me.

While I had money in the bank, I didn't flash money by wearing five-carat diamond earrings—instead I subtly made women aware of my wealth. Nearly every large purchase I made—from several homes, to luxury watches and vehicles—one of the women I was involved with at the time was usually present during the time of purchase. I relayed women to and from a beachside condo I had purchased in Florida and a multi-million dollar home I purchased in Colorado.

I surrounded myself with women who wanted me to be the man with whom they could establish a long-lasting relationship. Yet at the end of each day, I was simply paying for intimacy, sex, and companionship. In a sense, we were really just using each other. They used me for financial support, a trophy, or other benefits that came along with our involvement, and I used them for sex and companionship. I cannot think of one woman I purchased a gift for ever saying, "Wow. Thank you for the gift, but I can't and won't accept this." Or, "This is really nice of you Ian, but why all of this? What are your intentions?" In my heart I knew women were not disposable, but I treated them as if they were.

Despite the senseless, selfish, and seemingly heartless ways I dealt with women—as misguided as it was—I still had a *heart*. I truly desired to receive the love, trust, and respect of a woman. I longed for a woman who I could pray with—a woman who placed Christ above all else. I gained part of this insight during an encounter with one of my former teammates. In August of 2007, during the last two-a-day camp of my professional career, we traveled to Dallas to scrimmage the Cowboys for the week. As the week got underway, I began to smell retirement baking in the oven. My body had been through the grind of seven grueling two-a-days, with each passing day I was convinced that this, my eighth, would be my last.

One day, while kneeling on the sideline during the scrimmage, I saw a bright, beaming face walking toward me—my former teammate and also a strong brother in Christ. Becoming more and more disinterested in football by the minute, I grinned when I saw him. He greeted me with his usual, "Waz up, hero?" and I immediately smiled and stood to greet him. Speaking with him only for a moment, I felt so refreshed! After participating in a drill and returning to the sideline, I asked him about his wife.

"She's doing great, brother! In fact, you know what she said to me the other day?"

"No," I said, "but I wanna hear it."

Plant Water Grow

"Ian, she looked straight into my eyes and said, 'Baby, I love you so much! And you are my hero—number two!'"

"Woooow!" I said. "What a blessing to have a wife who truly loves and cares for you—but loves God more! I am so happy for you, man! Hearing that gives me hope that there is a godly woman out there waiting for me to find her. You just made my day!"

In the days, weeks, and months that followed I often thought back to his wife's comment. *I'm crazy to think I'll ever find a woman who can look me in the eye and say those words—because I know I'm not able to say the same.*

I knew what I wanted in a woman, but what type of man had I become? Toward the end of my NFL career, I began receiving words of encouragement and also of admonishment from three of my female cousins—Darchell, Kineta, and Fe'neda. God used these women to subtly—sometimes directly—convict me of my battle with sex. Whether I spent time with them in person or on the phone, I tried—rather unsuccessfully—to hide my struggle. Talking with my cousins made me extremely ashamed of the way I used and treated women. In fact, I would always coach the women I introduced to my cousins on how to conduct themselves, knowing my cousins could discern my own lustful nature from a mile away. But, the unconditional love my cousins offered me comforted me. The conversations and time spent with them also had another effect—

they allowed me a much-needed chance to witness the purity and holiness of Godly women.

In addition to conversations with my cousins, there were several encounters with some of my younger teammates that also helped keep my mind sober. While I often tried to share some advice from personal experience—whether with football or life—I was usually the one who ended up walking away more enlightened and convinced that life was so much bigger than chasing women and playing football. This was especially the case with one particular interaction.

Just before practice one day, I over heard one of the rookies sharing his financial struggles with another teammate. He had used his entire practice squad salary to take care of his wife, children, and mother. I took a seat next to him.

"Hey, if you need anything—anything at all—let me know, okay?"

"Oh nah, I'm cool," he said proudly, "But thanks, Ian!"

Despite all of my frivolous spending, whenever I saw or heard of a person in need, I often felt compelled to help in whatever capacity I could. After extending the offer I got up and walked away. A few months passed by and Christmas drew near. I found myself sitting next to him one day in the locker room and he whispered, "Hey, were you serious when you said you would help me out?"

"Yah," I replied. "What's up?"

"Well, Christmas is coming up and I don't have the money to get gifts for my wife, kids or my mother. So um, I was wondering if—"

"Man," I replied, while cutting him off in mid sentence, "How much do you need?"

"Whatever you want to give me," he humbly replied, "I'll pay you back when—"

"Dude, you're not paying me back. Just be sure to help someone in need when you can."

The next day without a word, I slid him a check in the locker room, then walked away.

The week after Christmas, I entered a hotel dining room the morning before the last game of my final NFL season, and this particular teammate was sitting at a table alone eating his breakfast. Noticing he was alone, I grabbed a plate of food and sat down with him. Suddenly, he looked up at me and said, "Oh, Ian, my mama wanted me to tell you thank you for the bed."

"Huh?" I replied. "What are you talking about?"

"Oh, my mama has never had a bed. She's always slept on an air mattress on the floor," he explained. "With some of the money you gave me, I bought her a bedroom set and gave it to her for Christmas!"

Hearing his words, my heart broke with compassion.

After our conversation, he got up and left the room—taking my appetite with him. I walked back up to my hotel room in total shock from what he told me, grabbed my phone, and called my mother. As I began to share what I had just heard, tears began to fall down my face as my heart went out to him and his mother. Hearing his story of Christmas reminded me how rewarding it is to be used by God. Despite all my frivolous spending, God allowed me to help a young man purchase his mother's very first bed.

Somewhere underneath my ego, my cold and lustful nature, the little boy who grew up longing and willing to offer unconditional love and acceptance to those in need still lived. Somewhere between praying to God while kneeling on my bedroom floor as a child and becoming a Pro Bowl Linebacker in the NFL, I lost my "true" identity—an identity firmly rooted in a seed of goodness, which was planted within me while helping a blind man cross the street at the age of eleven. I was like a lone eagle soaring majestically through the sky, with absolutely no direction. But, no matter how morally lost or how far I strayed from God, I never forgot that His hand was upon me, and that I was destined to fulfill His divine purpose—a destiny established even before the day of my conception. Up to this point in my life the question, *Lord, why did you create me?*, never entered my mind. As I grew more and more tired of running away from God, however, for the first time in my life I slowed down just enough to *acknowledge* Him.

One beautiful Florida morning in April of 2008, the words of my grandfather were heavy on my heart—"Never stop acknowledging God." After getting out of bed and opening up my blinds, I decided to spend some time thanking God for His existence and presence in my life. I turned on some praise and worship music and began a sincere and desperate prayer.

"Lord, let there be a paradigm shift in my life—"

Suddenly, God interrupted me.

"No! There needs to be an eternal shift in your life because you are headed to the lake of fire!"

The moment I heard those words—and roots from the seed of God's love began to dig into the deepest depth of my heart; I knew I had a choice to make. Immediately falling to my knees and weeping before the Lord, *my heart finally turned to God.* This day marked my complete and total surrender to Christ.

In complete contrast to what I had experienced during my days of playing football on national television, there was no applause for the single *greatest moment of my life*. Through my weeping, I heard no cheers from screaming fans or dancing cheerleaders. Not one camera or reporter surrounded me in the moment of my surrender to Christ. Before an audience of One, I surrendered my life, my control, my will, and all of my possessions to the Lord. Falling to my face, I spent the next hour or so lying on the ground before the

Lord weeping and crying my heart out, as I thought of how unworthy and undeserving I was to receive His undying love—the very love that consoled and comforted me in my greatest times of need.

Subsequent to my surrender, consumed by God's unconditional love for me, with all my heart I chose to profess Jesus as Lord and believe that God raised Him from the dead. In doing so I received the gift of salvation. Upon receiving God's eternal salvation, He removed the seed of guilt that the devil had planted inside me long ago, and replaced it with a seed of justification.

Now you may be wondering, "How did you obtain *salvation* without being inside of a building full of believers or without a pastor or minister present?" The answer is simple, the Apostle Paul writes,

> *If you declare with your mouth, "Jesus is Lord," and believe in your heart that God raised him from the dead, you will be saved. For it is with your heart that you believe and are justified and it is with your mouth that you profess your faith and are saved (Romans 10:9-10, niv).*

Notice in the above passage that there is no mention of a need to be inside of a building, or to be in the presence of a pastor, minister, or any other person for Jesus Christ to save someone. No, in spite of all of the superstitious prayers and rituals that people—even some pastors and ministers—

Plant Water Grow

practice and subscribe to, I received salvation in the privacy of my own home by simply confessing with my mouth that "Jesus is Lord" and believing in my heart that God raised Him from the dead. Jesus Christ did not come to the earth to judge, destroy, or condemn us. Jesus came to save each of us, and take away all of our sins through His suffering, His death, and His resurrection (John 12:47).

Immediately following my surrender, I felt like I was standing at the edge of the rest of my life. And there, for the first time ever, I could clearly see what I had done with my life up to that moment—what type of person I had become and where I was headed—and I didn't like what I saw. Sure, I had earned my college degree, had spoken to groups of young people in an effort to encourage them to make the right choices in life, earned a great deal of money—of which I gave very generously. I even attended Sunday morning services on occasion. Yet, sin was just as much—if not even more of—a part of my everyday life, as I committed acts of idolatry, sexual immorality and deception on a daily basis.

Up to this point in my life, I hadn't made much effort to help make the people around me, or the world I lived in, better. I had become a man lost in a world of his own selfish desires, and I knew that if I continued along this same path, I would be lost forever. I was a man obsessed with sleeping with a countless number of women, most of whom I hardly knew. I listened and answered to no one. I had in a way become a god to myself. The devil did a tremendous job of persuading me to rely on my intellect and confidence, my strength and courage, my good looks, charm, and swagger. Yet after realizing God had grown tired of my deceptive, wasteful, and selfish nature, I embraced my inferiority, my weakness, and my brokenness before Him.

In admitting my failure as a man, I acknowledged His strength and saving power. And in doing so, I became a real man—a man of God.

Despite finally feeling as though I was in right standing with God, all of my worries and struggles didn't just miraculously disappear. The "deep seeded" roots of lust, deception and promiscuity were still very much alive—and in the weeks, months, and years that followed, I still chased and deceived women.

My spirit was willing, but my flesh was weak.

You see, although the choice I made in my heart on the day of my surrender caused a shift to my "spiritual man," it would take years for that shift to manifest itself fully in my "natural man"—my flesh, my mind and body. There was still a great deal for me to learn.

Soon after my surrender, God said, "I am not concerned about you committing sin. Rather, my focus is now zoomed in on the true desire of your heart. Will your heart turn from me if you commit a sin? Will you abandon your pursuit of my righteousness if you fall into temptation? Or will you get up, dust yourself off and continue pursuing my righteousness?"

It wasn't long before I hurried back home to Michigan to share the good news of my surrender with my grandparents, knowing they had both been praying for this day to come! The moment I told Grandma and Papa, they both offered me words of wisdom and encouragement. My grandmother embraced me.

"I'm glad fo' ya!" she said. "Now you just trust in the Lord because He'll keep ya!"

Papa chimed in, "I'm glad fo' ya, too! You betta' believe He'll keep ya!"

I truly enjoyed spending time with both of them. Each time I went home to Michigan, I loved nothing more than finding a seat close to my grandfather—who picked cotton in the fields of Mississippi as a young man and had since been ministering the gospel—all in hopes of gleaning wisdom from him.

He would often say, "Ian, hane me dat Bible."

"Okay, Papa. This one?"

"Naw," he said. "Da other one."

"Um, this one?"

"Naw, da blue one."

Papa had hundreds of Bibles. After finally locating the correct Bible, he would instruct me which scripture to read. Then he'd share wisdom and insight he had gained from the Lord about the passage. There were also several times when I'd ask him questions about life. One day I worked up the nerve to ask him something I'd wondered since my teenage years.

"Papa," I asked, "it's always seemed easier to live a life of sin than to live righteously. Can you please help me understand?"

Being a man of great wisdom, he replied in a tone full of love and compassion, "Well, if ya put a man in a car and let 'im drive down da road, and den da man wit' the flashin' lights pull up behin' 'im, if da man has done sum'n wrong—what you thank he gon' do?"

"He'll probably panic and speed off, or try to get away from the police somehow," I replied.

"Yaahh," he said gently. "Na, take anudda man and put 'im in a car, and he go drivin' down da road and da man wit' da lights pull up behin' 'im, but dis man ain't done nuttin' wrong—what you thank *he* gon' do?"

"Slow down and pull over."

"You betta' believe it!" he laughed!

Hearing my grandfather's words—while a seed of understanding was planted within me—it finally dawned on me, *As a result of the bad choices I've made, I've been living a life full of anxiety and fear!* I had been constantly fearful of the negative consequences I could potentially face due to my foolish actions. Unlike David in Psalms 23:4, though *I* walked through the valley of the shadow of death, I *feared* all kinds of evil—*I wonder if she uses protection with other guys because she never asks me to use any. I hope she isn't the stalker type. I hope she doesn't have an STD. Please don't let her fall in love with me. I hope her boyfriend doesn't find out. I hope she's really separated from her husband. I hope she doesn't get pregnant.*

I also experienced this fear and anxiety when I went to strip clubs, nightclubs, and bars. While standing in rooms crowded with people and loud music, random thoughts would race through my head—*They need to have metal detectors in here because some fool could have a gun. Why are those dudes looking at me? Maybe they want to rob me. Or maybe I slept with one of their girlfriends! Can I trust her enough to take her back to my place, or should I take her to a hotel? Why did I park in that dark alley?* Again, all my fear and anxiety came from doing things I had no business doing and being in places I had no business being! If I chose not to sleep around or be out late at night, there would have been no need for my anxiety. Sadly, *fear* became just as much a part of my life as the sex, lies, and deceit.

During another visit home to Michigan, my mother picked me up from the airport and she asked her usual question as she drove: "You wanna go over to Grandma's?"

"Yah," I responded, "Gotta go check on Grandma and Papa."

While I wanted to spend time with both of my grandparents, I was most excited to ask my grandfather a new question—a question I had never asked anyone before.

Upon entering their modest three-bedroom home, I greeted my grandmother, and immediately asked, "Where's Papa?"

"Chil' he back there layin' down."

After making my way down a short hallway, I lightly knocked on the bedroom door. Papa immediately pushed the covers back and sat up on the side of his bed to greet me. We embraced warmly and then I sat next to him as he began to minister to me about the Lord. While he spoke, sensing the presence of God in the room, I could no longer contain my urge to ask my question! So I asked slowly, "Papa, I was wondering if you would be willing to pray for me."

"Yaahh, I be glad to pray fo' ya!" he said.

I slid down the side of the bed until my knees reached the hardwood floor. While kneeling before my grandfather, he gently placed both of his hands on my shoulders and—as a seed of humility was planted within me—he prayed for me.

This was the very first time in my entire life that I willingly humbled myself before another man. And in doing this, I embraced my desire to fully submit to Christ. It was also an admission of my need to receive counsel and guidance from a man of God. In that moment, Ian Gold, the arrogant and womanizing NFL linebacker, fell crashing to his knees to receive prayer and blessing from a man who was a father of twelve, a senior pastor, and an elder who spent the majority of his time—both day and night—praying for the lost, the sick, and the needy. A Godly man who grew up picking cotton in the fields of Mississippi and who lived eighty-nine long years to tell me all about it!

In the days following my grandfather's prayer, I spent more and more time thinking about God's purpose and plan for my life. During a flight to my condo in Florida, God told me to take out my laptop and begin typing—so I did. Here are the words that came out:

There are people who live life and never fully understand God's love. I am guilty. For almost thirty years I have lived in such a place of uncertainty and doubt. I look back at my childhood and see my parents fighting and arguing, my dad leaving for weeks, months, and even years at a time—only returning when he saw fit. But it wasn't all bad. In spite of it all, my mother was strong and courageous enough to eventually walk away—with four baby boys and only two arms.

I look back at my youth and I see myself angry and bitter, reaching out for love and affection only to receive punishment for my misbehavior. I learned to be alone as I felt exiled from everything and everyone I trusted to love me. My dad was non-existent. My mother was so preoccupied that her time was divided. And there was a division between my older brothers and me that I blamed myself for because I thought something was wrong with me.

I look back at my late teenage years and early 20's and I see the makings of what I had thought a good man. I was helpful, giving, loving, and a hard worker—filled with ambition and determination to achieve whatever level of success God would allow. I even thought I truly loved the Lord. Boy, was I wrong!

I look back over the past six or seven years of my life and see darkness—so much of it that I can't see others. But I hear people weeping. I see myself as a man who never truly allowed God to use him.

But now I am walking on a new path and there is no more darkness! The clouds are gone and the light is shining so bright, I cannot even see my hands in front of me! I see others walking in the light! There is so much comfort and warmth. It is consuming me more and more each day!

I met Grace and Mercy and asked them where they had been all my life, and they replied, "God only allows us to reside in the light—we are forbidden to go into the darkness."

"How did I get here?" I asked.

"It was I who brought you here," I heard someone answer. It felt as though God had breathed on me!

I looked and Grace and Mercy were gone from my presence and I stood there alone. Then I heard the same voice again, "I am God's Love and I brought you here with me. Only I can travel in both the light and the darkness. God sends me when a child is lost in the darkness. I am wherever God wants me to be. I have been with God since the beginning and will be with Him until everlasting. I was there with Jesus Christ on the cross, just as I have been with you all of your life. I am God's Love."

So why did Grace and Mercy go away? I thought.

"I sent you Grace and Mercy to comfort you, for they come from me," God's Love answered.

"Can you stay with me forever?" I asked, weeping.

"I am with you always. Nothing can separate you from me!" He responded.

To God be the glory for His Love! Amen.

This pierces my heart every time I read it because I believe it contains the very essence of God's *loving* nature. Sitting on the airplane flight to Florida, after reading what I wrote, I distinctly heard God say, "Ian, I created you for my divine purpose and equipped you with everything you need to fulfill my purpose for your life. I have given you love, faith, knowledge, wisdom, resources, a loving and supportive family—all you need to fulfill my divine purpose for your life. It's like the man who invented the light switch never turning it on, the man who invented the typewriter never putting paper in it, or the man who invented the oven never putting any food in it—all of these inventions would be absolutely *useless* if they were not used for the purpose they were created. In the same way, you have been *useless* to me because you have not allowed me to use you for the purpose I have created you for."

After hearing God's words, I began to weep.

I turned toward the window to hide my tears from the woman sitting next to me. I felt as though God was preparing to take His love away from me. *What?!? The same God who created me just told me I was useless to Him?*

The heartache of letting God down was unbearable. It was worse than any I had experienced before. But then I thought, *Wait, I haven't been totally useless, have I? What about all of the women I purchased Bibles for? What about the house I bought my mom? And what about all of the people I've shared the gospel with or given money to? Surely that counts for something, right?*

"Everything you did for others," God said in response, "edified them and allowed their faith in me to increase. You, however, were still headed to the lake of fire!"

Hearing these words, I began grieving with all of my heart and soul for the innocent little boy who was buried deep down inside of me. But then, I suddenly felt an overwhelming sense of peace—as if God Himself had embraced me.

"You are still alive," God said.

In that moment, no longer focused on my own selfish desires, I desperately pleaded with the Lord to give me one more chance to be useful to Him.

Lord, I silently pleaded, *you can take away everything—the houses, money, cars and women—but please give me just one more chance to be useful to you!*

As the plane landed safely, I pulled myself together and attempted to wipe away any evidence of my encounter with God.

Two weeks after my encounter on the airplane, God responded to my plea.

"Okay, I am going to give you a chance to be useful to me. I want you to create a website, and with this website I want you to capture the innocent and profound nature of my children—their pure and innocent thoughts are the most valuable resource on the planet!"

Gladly accepting my first assignment from above—as a seed of God's purpose for my life was planted inside me—with more intensity and enthusiasm than I played the game of football with, I went after my chance to become useful to God! In no time at all, I hired an interactive agency to build WhatAreKidsSaying.com (WAKS)—a website that allows kids and teens to express themselves through creative writing, as well as receive helpful advice and consultation. Shabnum Sheikh, MD, my mother's best friend from college that kindly let me live in her basement, graciously donates her time to respond to questions from WAKS members. In October 2008, WAKS was officially launched. Immediately following the launch of WAKS, I asked, "I built the website, God. Now what do you want me to do?"

"Now I want you to travel around the country," he replied, "and share the testimony of your salvation with young people. You have become a witness to young men and women who don't understand my purpose for their lives. Encourage them to put their trust in me and not in man. And be sure to tell them that I am always here for each of them—just as I have always been there for you."

Filled with gratitude, I humbly accepted God's next assignment—and in January 2009, I began my travels. God instructed me to pay for all of my own expenses—airline tickets, hotel rooms, and informational material. He also instructed me not to receive any payment for speaking, since the opportunity to be used by Him was more than enough payment! Throughout the course of the entire year I visited over thirty different high schools, middle schools, churches, and juvenile detention centers. My travels took me to New York, Florida, California, South Carolina, Illinois, Georgia, as well as several cities in Michigan and Colorado. I was also invited to be the keynote speaker at a number of conferences and events. I spoke to young people about life and the challenges I faced as I tried so desperately to become successful.

During my travels I grew accustomed to answering the same questions. One day, however, while speaking to a group of middle school students in Colorado, a young girl asked me a question that shook me to my very core.

"How did you deal with not having your dad around?"

The moment I heard her question, my heart flooded with pain. Tears welled up in her tiny eyes, and roots from the seed of compassion pierced my heart. When I tried to respond to her question, I paused as I choked up. As my eyes traveled around the classroom I noticed her teacher wiping tears from her eyes, and I nearly lost my composure altogether. Standing in front of the small group of students, while sensing her longing for her dad just as I did at her age, I somehow managed to fight back my tears. All I really wanted to do was walk over to her, give her a big hug, and let her know that she had a Father in heaven that she could *always* depend on.

I had judged my dad my whole life for his faults and many indiscretions, but in doing so I became blinded to my own. Did he force me to steal candy from the corner drug store when I was twelve? Did he coerce me into having sex with so many women that I lost count back in college? No, I made those decisions all on my own! In recognizing this truth, I knew I could no longer judge him.

And so, in 2008, after nearly seven years of not speaking to my dad, I decided to call him up and ask him to forgive me for all of the disrespect I had shown him over the years. Following my apology, we decided to wipe the slate clean.

Since then, we have been on a journey—albeit a slow one—back toward establishing a loving relationship. The moment I stopped judging my dad—then and only then—was I able to begin letting go of all of the anger, bitterness, hurt, and pain which was stored up inside of me for over twenty years. I finally began dealing with my own indiscretions—and a seed of responsibility had been planted inside me.

The growing pains of this decision first surfaced as I spoke to a group of young people at a retreat in Georgia. As I talked to them about the subject of dating, I began to paint a picture of the man I used to be. I shared with them how I lied to and deceived women, entering into sexual relationships with no regard for these women whatsoever. Then suddenly, after the picture of the man I was, had become clearly visible to me, I paused—and the tears began to fall. The thought of my actions were too painful to think of. Through the tears, however, I continued painting the picture, as I desperately wanted my experiences to help each of the young men and women choose a path different from the one I chose at their age.

When God told me I was useless, it was as if He had said, "Ian, you have been useless with the life I have given you, so it's time for your death." *Please, give me one more chance to be useful*, I desperately cried out. And he did—God spared my life. Which is why the life I live today is surrendered to Him.

CHAPTER 9
CHASING HORIZONS

There's an old saying that goes, "Old habits die hard," and nothing could be truer of my life. Sadly, after surrendering my life to Christ, I continued "chasing horizons." My battle with sex continued, as several women made their way in and out of my life. By this time in my life, the tiny seed of lust that was planted inside me on the day of my first kiss had blossomed into a sexual and deceptive nature that resulted in a number of broken hearts—including my own.

In the fall of 2006, before my surrender to Christ, I began a sexual relationship with a woman even though I was involved with several other women at the time. My relationship with her, like many of the others, was on and off. Although I didn't want to be seriously involved with her, I enjoyed her company. In fact, during the summer of 2007, after telling me about her plans to backpack through Europe with her best friend, I agreed to meet up with them in London. I booked a suite large enough for all of us, which included a room for her and me and a separate room for her best friend. At the time it felt pretty good to visit another country and have a half naked woman waiting for me in my hotel room. To hop on a plane, fly to London, or any city I was scheduled to play in, and have sex with a woman upon arriving at my hotel, had simply become another expression of my purpose*less* lifestyle. As a professional athlete it was what society expected of me, and sadly enough, it had become all I expected of myself.

While in London, we enjoyed our time touring the city—Buckingham Palace, Big Ben, London Square, and we enjoyed several long walks. We also found time to attend a theater production, dine out at a few of London's popular restaurants, purchase some artwork, even share a dance in the middle of a crowded bar one evening. After the fun was over, however, I headed south to Barcelona alone, and they continued on to Amsterdam.

The next time I saw her was at the beginning of 2009, at my house in Colorado. She came over to late one night to "watch a movie"—but by the time she left she probably felt as though she had played a role in one.

Following her arrival to my place, and learning that I had a massage room, I offered her a massage and we wound up being intimate. After getting sexually reacquainted with one another, we decided to watch a movie. But, as we watched the movie, my front doorbell began ringing nonstop. I tried to ignore it, hoping she wouldn't hear it, but eventually she asked, "Um, is there someone at your door?"

"I don't know," I replied, "Let me go check."

Plant Water Grow

I slowly tip toed up my spiral staircase heading to the front door. *Who in the world is ringing my doorbell at ten o'clock at night? I live in a gated community!*

As I approached the top of the flight of stairs, the ringing stopped, but now someone was banging on my bedroom door. Then I heard it—the voice of my girlfriend of seven years yelling, "Ian, I know you're in there! You are such a liar! I'm not leaving until you come out here and show your face! You talk about God and the Bible and all of that stuff, but you're such a liar and a hypocrite!"

She was right and had every right to be upset. I was guilty of everything she said and, shamefully, so much more. As I quietly made my way back downstairs to the theater, hoping she would tire and go home, I told my guest that she had nothing to worry about.

The ringing, knocking, and banging persisted, however.

Noticing my company growing more and more uncomfortable, I went upstairs and headed straight for my bedroom door. I could hear my girlfriend complaining to her mother, "Mom, I'm so angry! I feel like a complete fool! I should have never trusted him!"

I opened the door.

She turned to me and asked, "So, what are you doing? Whose car is that in your driveway?"

Quickly thinking of a good lie to tell her, I responded, "Relax. A friend of mine is having some issues with her boyfriend, so I invited her to come over and talk. Then we decided to watch a movie downstairs in the theater, so I didn't hear you knocking."

What made this situation worse was the fact that I had just spoken to her about an hour or so before and made it appear as if I was going to sleep—so she wasn't buying the lie at all.

"Okay. Then let me come in and talk to her."

"Look," I responded firmly, "you're obviously very angry and upset and she's scared of what you might do to her—so I'm sorry, but I can't let you go down there.'

She left very angry and upset. Meanwhile, "the other woman" found herself smack in the middle of my latest drama. Wanting no part of it, she left minutes after my girlfriend sped off in her car.

Although I talked a good game, I was miserably failing to practice what I preached when it came to integrity with women. In every other area of my life, I had integrity, but when it came to women, I was a master of deception and lies. While I didn't drink, use drugs, or break any laws, regretfully I did use and emotionally abuse women.

Out of a group of women I was involved with simultaneously, I witnessed the destruction of the innocence of two women. One of them was my girlfriend of seven years, who I just mentioned. I met her in the fall of 2002 at a nightclub in downtown Denver. When we met, she said she wanted to take

Plant Water Grow

things slowly because she had just gotten out of a painful relationship. Once I got to know her, I decided not to rush, exercising some patience for once in my life. In fact, I waited three *whole* weeks to have sex with her, which felt like a lifetime—the longest period of time I ever waited for a woman during my NFL career.

Even though I told her I wanted to be in a committed relationship, after we had sex the first time, I maintained casual sexual relationships with other women throughout our entire seven year relationship, including a professional cheerleader I met during training camp for the Buccaneers in 2005. I had been isolated from women for weeks, and one day I noticed a table full of cheerleaders in the hotel dining room. I thought, *It's about time I get to see some women! I wonder why none of the fellas are sitting over there. Oh well, less competition for me.*

Confidently taking my seat at the table, I introduced myself, immediately setting my sights on one of them. Much to my disappointment, however, it was rumored that she had already had sex with a number of my teammates—so I stopped pursuing her. But I was determined to have sex with at least one of them, and after exchanging phone numbers with one of them during a night out in a local casino, we soon began a sexual relationship that spanned two and a half years.

At the time, I was committing crimes worse than grand larceny. As I robbed women of the affection and admiration that should have been reserved for their future husbands—while carelessly giving away what I should have reserved for my future wife. Of all the women I became sexually involved with, both, my girlfriend and the cheerleader from Tampa followed my example, becoming involved with multiple sexual partners. They gave me a spoon full of my own medicine—and I didn't like it! Their deception and lies hurt me, but what else could I have expected? Nothing. I had no right to be upset with them for doing what I had done to countless women for years. As the distance grew between them and me, my cold heart began to thaw—and for the first time I suffered the pain of loss. Yet before losing them both, they became victims of what would prove to be my greatest work of deception—conceiving a child with a woman I hardly knew.

Surprised and shocked by this news, these two women were devastated, knowing that it could have been either one of them. In fact, at one point they each told me, "Ian, that should have been us."

Then came the judgment.

"Ian, you're a ho!" the cheerleader from Tampa blurted out during a heated phone conversation.

She was right. But who was she to judge me? Needless to say, our conversation did not end well.

Did I set out to become a ho. Not at all. Nor did I want to date a ho. But, that is exactly what I was, and exactly what

Plant Water Grow

these two women and many others, who I became sexually involved with, became.

With the distance growing between each of these women and myself, a seed of truth was planted within me—and God began to teach me some valuable lessons. One day I heard God say, "All sex before marriage does is create a false sense of ownership."

This totally contradicted my ideas and beliefs. You see, I actually believed that having sex with women meant they did belong to me. I was horribly mistaken. At the time, if I would have ever paused and picked up a Bible, I would have clearly seen how God instructs us to refrain from sexually immoral behavior, which means that any form of sex outside of marriage is an abomination to God—as sex is *only* acceptable in the eyes of God when it is between a man and a woman within the sanctity of marriage. Needless to say, my words and actions, at the time, were in direct contradiction to God's instructions. In fact, I remember saying to a few of my teammates, *The women I date are all like dogs on leashes—if I let one go, I simply go pick the leash up again.* Until one day the cheerleader from Tampa ran away from me and directly into the arms of Jesus.

What amazed me about her decision is that, prior to her running away from me, she had a startling answer to a question I asked one day while we were lying in bed. I asked,

"If you were stranded on an island and you could only choose one person to be with you, would you choose me or Jesus?"

"Both!" she cheerfully replied.

Dissatisfied with her answer I asked her the question repeatedly. However, after hearing the same answer again and again, I silently prayed, *Lord please allow her to choose you above all else, including me.*

It's funny how when God finally answered my prayer, I became jealous. The fierce competitor within me wanted her back! And as I attempted to win her heart again, I distinctly remember hearing from the Lord, "She does not belong to you. She belongs to me. And so do you!"

After hearing this, I was repentant, feeling ashamed and disgraced by my attempt to "win her away from the Lord." *Please forgive me, Lord, for thinking she, or any other woman, ever belonged to me.*

You see, back when Adam was in the garden of Eden, he was never *possessive*. In fact, the thought of owning or possessing *any* of God's creations never entered his heart or mind. In other words, he never looked at Eve and said, "Okay, this is my section of the garden—and that's yours," or "Eve, God gave you to me, so you have to do whatever I tell you to do." Instead, Adam and Eve lived with one another in perfect harmony. What I realize today, is that my thoughts of controlling and possessing women had resulted from my ignorance and lack of understanding about their true value.

Plant Water Grow

Following my last meaningful communication with that cheerleader from Tampa, and despite all of my deception and lies, I became "semi-engaged" to my girlfriend from Denver—the one I had been dating for seven years. By semi-engaged, I mean the ring I purchased for her stayed locked up in a drawer in my office because I knew that once I gave it to her, there would be no turning back. But, after seven long years of listening to all of my empty promises of us living "happily ever after," my hesitation to give her the engagement ring was enough for her to end our relationship for good.

A few weeks after she ended our relationship, I saw her out at an event one evening. In my effort to gain her sympathy, I forced a few tears to fall. When I realized she was not buying my pathetic and disingenuous act, I decided to leave. Ironically, somewhere along my drive home a flood of genuine and painful tears arose from the depths of my heart. Did I miss her? Certainly. But, having never shed a tear over a woman before, I immediately asked God why I was so overwhelmed with emotion.

God then showed me all of the heartache and pain I had caused her and also many other women over the years, and for the first time ever I felt the pain, hurt, and heartache I had caused. It was nearly unbearable. When I finally made it home I found myself on my knees in the middle of my closet weeping for all of the women I had hurt. I firmly believe that God wanted me to feel this pain and suffering so that I would understand what I had done to so many women over the years.

The next day, I called my mother on the phone. Sensing my heavy heart, she said, "It's time for you to stop being so hard on yourself. The one thing you need to know is: *women know*. Ian, these women you were involved with may have pretended they had no idea what you were up to—*but they knew!* Even more, they willingly chose to stay involved with you for their own selfish reasons."

My mother made a great point—I needed to stop beating myself up and instead learn from my mistakes and move on. Following our conversation, I was determined to do my best not to give history an opportunity to repeat itself. *Why did I lie to women? Why couldn't I just let women move on with their lives, especially knowing I wasn't ready for a commitment? Why would I ask for her hand in marriage if I had never seriously done so in the seven years we dated?*

Traveling across the country speaking to young people gave me plenty of time to search for answers, until finally one day it dawned on me. *I've been a coward!* A true gentleman once said to me on a flight, "My father told me that any man can sleep around with multiple women, but the strongest and truest of men are able to remain faithful, loyal, and committed to one woman." Surprisingly, this was the first time I had ever heard such a statement. In time, I fully embraced his remark

Plant Water Grow

as a word from God, prompting me to change my wrongful and careless way of thinking.

Many of the relationships and love affairs I have been involved in over the years have been meaningless, pointless, and simply a waste of *time*. Due to my selfish and obsessive nature, I robbed women of their precious time and God's purpose for allowing us to meet. The issue of wasting time has always been a challenge for me. In the fifth chapter of Ephesians, verses 15-16, the Apostle Paul says,

> *See then that ye walk circumspectly, not as fools, but as wise, redeeming the time, because the days are evil.*

Paul is emphasizing the importance of using time wisely, as we are living in evil days and there is no time for us to waste. Unfortunately, it's always been easy for me to diminish the value of time.

I remember nights when I was in grade school that, instead of washing the dishes, I chose to play video games with my brothers. Then I'd go to bed. And as soon as I fell into a good, deep sleep my mother would wake me up.

"Ian!" My mother would shout. "Didn't I tell you to wash these dishes?"

"Yeeessss." I shouted, with sleep in my voice.

"Well then, get yo' behin' down here and clean 'em, *now!*"

"But Mom, it's three o'clock in the morning and I have to get up to go to school in a few hours," I complained.

"I know!" She firmly replied. "You should've thought about that before you took yo' behin' to bed without doing what I told you to do! Now *get up* and come wash these dishes, *now*!"

Sleepy eyed and fully convinced my mother had completely lost her mind, I hunched over the kitchen sink and washed the dishes in the wee hours of the morning.

And how could I ever forget having little or no regard for the value of time in college. One night, instead of studying for a huge final exam I had the next day, I chose to go to a party with my friends. As a result, I failed the final exam, not only earning speeches from my head coach, my athletic academic advisor, and the Associate Vice Provost—but I also ended up on academic probation for the second time!

I also diminished the value of time by wasting it with a number of women I knew I had no business being with at all! Dating back to the summer before my freshmen year in college, I cannot begin to calculate all of the time I wasted with women—countless hours eating, being intimate, and talking on the phone. But I am finally beginning to learn how precious and valuable time truly is. Take the two hours I spent in Chicago one summer, for example.

One beautiful Sunday afternoon in downtown Chicago, I walked out of my hotel on a quest to find some Chicago style pizza. Serenaded by the "Chicago Inner-City Traffic Orchestra," I roamed the crowded streets on my quest. While watching people buzz from one side of the street to the other, in and out of the luxury boutiques and shops, I spotted a pizza restaurant. As my mouth began to salivate, I noticed a man lying down on the sidewalk. Immediately, my focus shifted. *Is he alive? I wonder if he's hungry?*

I slowed down my pace to watch him and the responses of other passersby—to my amazement, person after person walked right by him with absolutely no regard. *I guess they didn't have the time.* Standing near him, I asked,

"Hey! Hey bro, you okay? Are you hungry? I'm about to go eat—and you can come with me if you want."

"What you goin' to eat?" he replied, as he sat up and used one hand to block the glare from the scorching sun.

"Pizza!"

"Man, I can't eat that," he said. "I got stomach cancer."

I should ask him if I could pray with him, I thought, while inching closer to him.

Then he said, "Hey brutha, can you do something for me?"

"Sure, what is it?"

"Can you pray wit' me?"

I knew I was exactly where God wanted me to be.

"Of course," I replied and took a seat on the ground right next to him. As we sat and talked for the better part of an hour, he opened up and shared details about his life with me. At one point in the conversation he asked, "Can I tell you something?"

"Yah, I'm listening."

"Now," he said nervously, "when I tell you this, please don't judge me, man."

Assuring him I would not judge him and reminding him that we all have many faults and indiscretions of our own, he said, "Well, I just got out of jail six months ago—I spent twenty years in prison because I killed a man. At the time, I knew it wasn't the right thing to do, but...the man raped and murdered my little sister. So I did what I did and I paid the price for it."

"If you could go back in time, would you do it again?" I asked.

"No!" he blurted without hesitation. "Only God decides who lives and who dies."

Sensing his remorse and genuine heart, my respect for him grew.

"Man, people usually get up and walk away when they hear about what I did."

"Who am I to judge you?" I responded.

"Man, you know what I do while I'm out here on these streets? I talk to the kids who walk by me every day and I tell them to keep God first and always listen to their mothers and fathers."

Wow! I thought in amazement. *God allowed me to create a website to benefit the lives of young people, and here I am, sitting next to a homeless man, and God is allowing him to benefit their lives as well.*

Moments later, while in mid-conversation, he noticed a family approaching and said, "Hold on a second." Then he shouted, "Hey kids! Keep God first and always listen to your mother and father."

Just as the encouraging words came out of his mouth, I noticed the father pull his young child away from where we were sitting. But then, after realizing what the man sitting on the sidewalk had just said, although delayed, the father turned and smiled. "Thank you," he said politely.

Then, without skipping a beat, the man started right back in where he left off in our conversation. We talked for a while longer and finally shared a moment of prayer. I handed him a fist full of money that I had intended to give to my younger brother. His eyes lit up.

"*Aw, man!*" he exclaimed. "You know what I'm about to do?"

"What?" I asked.

"Buy me some new shoes!"

"Hey, there's a shoe store right around the corner, you wanna go?" I asked as we both stood up.

"Man, they not gon' let me in there."

"You're with me! Let's go!"

As we walked around the corner, he spotted someone he knew. "Wait a minute." He made his way back to the individual and without a word, handed him some of the money. When he returned, he said, "That's how it works—when God blesses you, you have to be a blessing to someone else!"

His kind gesture touched my heart and I fell in love with him all the more. As we walked into the store, his eyes opened wide and he removed the old dirty baseball cap from his head, unveiling the child-like expression written on his face! It was the same child-like expression that danced on the faces of women I treated to shopping sprees at high-end boutiques and department stores. But this time it was different—it tapped and waltzed itself all over his entire being!

Then he sped into action. Once we found him a pair of shoes, I encouraged him to get an outfit and a new baseball cap. Making our way to the cash register, he asked, "You think they'll let me wear my new stuff out of here?"

"Sure," I said, shrugging my shoulders. "I don't see why not!"

Standing at the cash register, I asked the cashier if she could get him a fitting room.

"Of course," she said. After he went inside the dressing room, she asked me, "So, how do you guys know each other?"

"Oh, we're brothers."

"Well, I don't really see the resemblance."

"We're all brothers and sisters in the body of Christ." I responded.

"Yah, that's true!" she replied, handing me my receipt.

Coming out of the fitting room wearing his new outfit, I could hardly recognize him. The man I discovered lying on the sidewalk had disappeared. Before parting ways, I felt an angelic presence. Standing amidst the crowds of people and chaos on Michigan Avenue, we shared a hug as he said,

"Well my brother, I don't know if I'll ever see you again—but if I don't, I'll see you in Glory!"

Moments after walking away, I turned back to look for him.

He was gone.

Yep, he had to be an angel.

The wealth of knowledge, wisdom, and understanding I received from the two hours I spent with the "angel in Chicago" was far more valuable than any I ever received from all of the time chasing women over the years! Experiences like this one forever compel me to make the most of the remaining time I have left in this world.

My hope is that the remainder of my time is valuable and redeemed for the cause of Christ.

With my new understanding of the value of time, I slowly began to lose the desire to hunt and chase women. One evening the Lord said to me, "It's *not* all about the chase! An animal being chased by a lion is running away for fear of its life, not because it thinks it's cute to be chased! Satan has caused women to think it's flattering and endearing to be chased by men. Along the same lines, he has deceived men into thinking women love to be chased."

Upon hearing God's words, a seed of self-control was planted inside me.

These words prompted me to think of what Jesus had told Simon and Andrew in the first chapter of Mark, verse 17:

Come ye after me and I will make you to become fishers of men.

Climbing into bed that evening, I struggled with what the Lord had told me, *Lord, then what is the difference between fishing and chasing or hunting—because they seem very similar.* I fell asleep waiting for God's response.

The next day, God answered, "Jesus fished for men and women to save their souls, while the devil hunts and chases men and women to destroy and devour their souls."

The moment I heard God's words I knew it was truth. In the fifth chapter of 1 Peter, verse 8, Peter says,

Be sober, be vigilant; because your adversary the devil, as a roaring lion, walketh about seeking whom he may devour.

This truth reminds me of a woman I met who was visiting Denver from Oakland during my playing days. Unfortunately, it serves as another illustration of how my appetite for sex drove me to chase women at any and all cost.

After meeting a woman in a nightclub, we decided to meet up again the next day at a local shopping mall. As we browsed through a clothing store, an extremely beautiful woman captured my attention. No longer focused on my date, I thought, *I can't pass up this opportunity!* As we continued to walk through the store, my date became interested in an article of clothing, so I said, "Wow, I think that would look really good on you. You should go try it on."

My plan worked. As she headed for the dressing room, I was able to initiate the chase. I was even ready to give the sales lady a few extra items to have my date try on just to keep her occupied long enough for me to get the other woman's phone number. As it turned out, the other woman was with another man. That didn't stop me, though—if I didn't see a wedding ring on a woman's finger, she was fair game.

So, in a way similar to two lions courting one another in the wild, I entered her space, positioning myself directly behind her. I began by "innocently" commenting on her taste in an article of clothing she was admiring.

Suddenly, I heard: "Ian! So, what do you think?"

"Huh?" I said, startled. "Oh yeah, that looks good on you! I put some other things back there that I think you'll look really good in, too. Go try them on!" Giving me a half smile, she slowly turned back toward her dressing room. When I turned back to speak to the other woman, she had vanished! I quickly dashed over to the dressing room area and shouted,

"Hey, I have to run to get some cash out of the ATM. But I'll be right back!"

She paused. "Um, okay."

I didn't need any money—but once I started the chase, I rarely gave up or quit!

Leaving the store, I spotted my "prey" through the tall, grassy plain of people. I hurried after her, finally catching up with her and the guy who appeared to be her date.

"Pardon me. I don't mean any disrespect, but are you guys together?"

"No," she replied, "we're just friends. I'm just visiting from out of town."

"Okay, cool. Well, you left the store before I had an opportunity to ask you for your phone number. So, would it be okay if we exchanged numbers?"

"Um, aren't you with that girl?" she asked.

Swallowing hard, I replied, "Okay, look—honestly, I met her last night and this is our first time hanging out. I can only imagine how this must look, but when I saw you I realized I couldn't pass up an opportunity to get to know you."

Appreciating my honesty and seemingly flattered by my effort, she gave me her number and we parted ways. By the time I arrived back at the store, however, my date was waiting for me.

We walked out of the store in awkward silence, and then it came, "So, did you get her number?"

"Yeah." I said, shocked by her boldness. "You mad at me?"

"Ugh! Men are dogs! And yes, I'm mad at you! It really bothers me!" She continued, "I mean, I know we're not together, but dang! You couldn't even wait 'til you were alone?"

"You're right. I was wrong. I'm sorry." I replied. "But she was leaving—and I didn't know if I would ever see her again."

After a few more moments of awkward silence, she started to laugh. Although she was frustrated with me then, she and I eventually began a sexual relationship that spanned the course of a year or so.

A few days later, I returned to the store and purchased the sweater jacket I saw the woman from Oakland admiring. And after speaking with her and getting her address, I sent her the jacket—along with a handwritten letter. Following a few conversations we had over the phone, she accepted an invitation to attend our preseason game in San Francisco.

When I arrived at our hotel in the Bay area, I raced up to my room to change out of my suit and tie. I sprinted back downstairs to the lobby where I knew she would be waiting for me and I saw her—*She's even more beautiful than I remember!* We left the hotel and grabbed a bite to eat, after which she dropped me back off at the hotel. One of my teammates, who grew up in the Bay area, and I decided to ask our head coach if we could stay in Oakland after the game—as players were expected to fly back as a team.

"If we win you can stay," he said. "Just promise me you won't be late to practice on Wednesday."

Well, we won—so we got to stay!

Over the next few days, I began a sexual relationship with my new friend that lasted the next seven years.

I share this story to not just give another illustration of my obsession with sex, but to show how selfish and inconsiderate I was whenever I chased women. I had no concern for a woman's wellbeing, and I certainly didn't encourage or build them up in anyway. I cared very little about the condition of a woman's heart, mind, or soul, as I was more concerned about getting my own desires and needs met. Taking one look at this woman's golden skin, her hair full of a million curls, and her thick physique, I had only thought—*I have to have her.* Like a lion going after its prey, I had only one concern—satisfying my hunger.

Jesus didn't chase and hunt people—he *fished* for men and women in order to save their souls! Looking back, I cannot help but wonder, *How many souls have I damaged by hunting and chasing women down for sex?* It hurts my heart to realize all of the pain and hurt I have caused women. Since learning the difference between fishing and chasing, however, I finally made the commitment not to chase after another woman for the rest of my life.

Now whenever I sense the hunting lion rising up inside of me, I command the righteous lion within me to conquer him! In time, and only with the help of the Holy Spirit, I hope to become more like the image of Jesus Christ—a true "fisher of men."

CHAPTER 10
THE PAINFUL TRUTH

Following my surrender to Christ, when I was not preoccupied with a woman, I was often alone. On the days that I was able to resist the temptation to be with a woman, I would wake up, spend time in prayer, and talk on the phone with fellow believers about God's word. Then, after the first half of my day was over, I usually spent the remainder playing instruments and singing, or in some way or another, seeking God for more wisdom as I shared all of my thoughts and questions with Him. As a result, God began to shower me with His wisdom and understanding. Looking back over the past three years, my faith in Christ has increased dramatically. Along the way I have learned some hard lessons—letting go of anger, bitterness, and hatred, learning instead how to live in harmony. The greatest truths God has revealed to me, however, are in the areas of understanding His nature as well as the process of forgiveness.

Before my surrender to Christ, I only prayed to God when I needed an "A" on an exam or a paper, or for healing from a football injury, or for protection from harm while chasing women late into the night. There were also many times I prayed and asked the Lord not to allow me to conceive a child before I got married. And in His grace, God answered the majority of my prayer requests despite my disobedience to Him. Then one day, I met the woman who would give birth to my beloved daughter.

The following details regarding my involvement with her are in no way an attempt to vilify her, as I have grown to respect, honor and love her dearly. Rather, my goal is to illustrate how *my* sinful nature and actions nearly destroyed one of God's most precious gifts—my little princess.

During my last season with the Broncos, I met my daughter's mother one night at a bar in downtown Denver. We immediately began a sexual relationship, which spanned the next nine months. After we started having sex, she became one of the women who—when I wasn't with my girlfriend—I casually spent time with. If my girlfriend wasn't sleeping over, or if I wanted a woman to keep me company in the hotel the night before a game, all it took was a phone call.

Plenty of women had enjoyed the idea of my "celebrity" status and lifestyle—waiting in the tunnel for me after games, the shopping sprees, and the fancy restaurants. That being said, however, no woman had ever allowed their appetite for my money, possessions, or status to cause them to commit any acts—like intentionally getting pregnant.

Then I received a phone call from my daughter's mother one afternoon.

"Ian—I'm pregnant."

"Okay, congratulations!" I replied, thinking, *It can't be mine because you told me you were on the pill.*

To my surprise, she added, "Ian—it's yours."

When I asked her about her birth control, she responded, "Well, my doctor made a mistake and gave me a low dosage pill and it didn't work as well as the high dosage pill." Unfortunately, this turned out to be untrue, as I later learned the term "low dose" has nothing to do with the effectiveness of a birth control pill.

In the end, I received some relief when she said, "Don't get all worried about it, because I'm gonna take care of it."

"Well, how much is it gonna cost?" I asked.

"Two thousand dollars."

"Okay," the coward in me replied, "I'll bring you the cash." I was man enough to conceive a child, but not man enough to accept the responsibility of raising one.

I delivered her the money to pay for the abortion procedure a few hours later. But as time passed and I didn't hear from her again, I began to question her motives. But trusting in my ability to judge character, I dismissed my suspicions—*Nah, she wouldn't get pregnant for money.*

As the day of her procedure drew near, I finally talked to her on the phone and she blurted out, "Well, what are you going to do for me? I mean, I'm not doin' this for nothing! I have student loans to pay off and my car is falling apart. So, what are you willing to give me?"

My stomach turned upside down, as a seed of hatred was planted inside me. Her pregnancy was not a mistake at all. Sadly, her pregnancy was a means for her to gain financially. Thirteen years of dodging numerous pregnancy scares, my worst nightmare had finally come true! Fully convinced this was all about money, I wanted to get proof of her deception, so I played along.

"Okay, how much do you want?"

"Forty thousand," she replied.

"Twenty," I countered.

After agreeing on a figure, she sent me a text message with her banking information. I admitted in a later phone conversation that I wouldn't be sending her any money, and she shouted, "See! I knew you were never gonna give me the money and that's why I'm keeping it!"

Her admission pissed me off! I began insulting her in ways no man should ever insult a woman. In the process of hurling insults back and forth, I lied to her and told her I had another woman pregnant, hoping she would proceed with the abortion. She didn't buy it. As my insults watered the seed of hatred within me, I finally erupted, "You're the reason why men don't want to have daughters!" Knowing I crossed a line, with those words, I abruptly ended the conversation.

After I calmed down, I realized there was a chance that another man was the father of her child because we had each openly admitted to being sexually active with other people during the course of our sexual involvement. With that, I tried my best to put her completely out of my mind.

As the months passed by, I found myself going back to life as usual. I was still involved with my girlfriend of seven years—how I managed to hide all of this—as well as my many other indiscretions—from her, I will never know. But with the fear of being found out lodged in the back of my mind, I focused my attention solely on her. *There's no way God would allow any woman who would try to get paid for having an abortion be a mother—let alone the mother of my child!*

Even though I was angry and disgusted with my daughter's mother, there were two occasions I reached out to her during her pregnancy out of both genuine and selfish concern. I thought, *She's uneducated, doesn't have a penny to her name, and has no real guidance from her parents. I can't be heartless and leave her to suffer alone.* I genuinely felt sorry for her. At one point during her pregnancy, she admitted selling her clothes to get money to buy food and pay her bills, so I decided to pay for her to move back home with her family who lived in a small town about an hour and a half from Denver.

On the two occasions I saw her prior to my daughter's birth, we also had sex. Although I was angry with her and could never see myself involved with her on a serious level, sadly, I had become a expert at separating what I felt emotionally from what I wanted physically. Ironically, I felt sorry for her and I hated her at the same time.

During one of our visits I told her, "If you needed money, all you had to do was ask and I would have given it to you. You didn't have to go to the extent of bringing a child into this world for money!"

Following our last sexual encounter, which took place a few weeks prior to my daughter's birth, she said, "Just so you know, you don't have to worry about me keeping her away from you, because I would never do that to you. I would never keep her away from her father." What I didn't realize then was that all hell was about to break loose!

On the day of my daughter's birth, the small stream of anger and deceit that resulted in our daughter being conceived nine months earlier had become a raging river of hatred and hostility. Anxious to know the truth, immediately after witnessing my daughter's birth I asked one of the nurses if she could facilitate a DNA test—which infuriated my daughter's mother. A week later, the results proved I was indeed the father, and standing on opposite banks of the waters of deception, our feelings of hatred and bitterness toward each other grew immensely. She began to use our daughter as a pawn. If I didn't play by her rules, she wouldn't allow me to see our daughter.

My interaction with my daughter's mother worsened when I got engaged to my girlfriend. During a visit with my daughter, I informed her mother of my engagement. An argument over money ensued and she threatened to call the police if I didn't leave. So I decided to do what any responsible and concerned parent would do—I filed a petition for custody of my daughter with the state of Colorado.

Finally, after spending months of fighting for custody of our daughter in court and being forced to visit her in public libraries, hotel rooms, and even at a women's safe house where I was supervised by an armed guard, I walked away with every other weekend visitations and a few weeks of visitation during summer months. Upon hearing the court's decision, I thought, *How in the world could the court give her primary custody when she openly admitted to asking me for forty thousand dollars in exchange for aborting our daughter?* Knee-deep in the river of deception we created, I once again chose to judge, as my anger and bitterness blinded me from acknowledging my part in our daughter's near demise.

Speaking only for myself here, giving my daughter's mother the initial two thousand dollars to get an abortion, and then later negotiating a price to abort our daughter, makes me an accomplice to premeditated murder. The truth is, because of the selfish nature and actions of both of my daughter's parents, there might have never been a need for attorneys, diapers, baby clothes, or calculating child support because my little angel would have been robbed of her precious little life.

So how is it that I—clearly guilty of not wanting a child—could fight over her in court after she was born? This question is sobering and difficult for me to think about without shedding tears. Distracted by all of the drama that surrounded my daughter's entrance to this world, I lost sight of God's divine plan and purpose for her life—*a purpose that no amount of her father's money, or selfishness, could ever abort!*

Since my daughter's birth, I have suffered greatly. Through all that I have endured, I have learned some lessons, some at great cost—how to love and forgive people who intend to hurt me, what it means to suffer for the cause of Christ, and how to hold my peace and let God fight my battles for me.

In June 2010, I received a phone call from a police detective.

"Mr. Gold, do you know why I'm calling you today?"

"No, I don't, officer," I replied.

"Well, apparently there was an incident at your home a week or so ago involving you and your daughter."

"Are you kidding me?" I asked.

"No, I'm not."

I explained to him that my slapping my daughter's forearm because she failed to obey my instructions had caused the bruises on her forearm.

"Well, Mr. Gold, since you've been extremely helpful and straightforward with my investigation, I'm not going to send a car out to pick you up and have you booked. Just come down to the station and pick up the ticket and make sure you appear in court."

After thanking the detective for his leniency, I hung up the phone. *Send a car to pick me up? I've never been arrested in my entire life! Is this a joke?*

In hindsight, I could have corrected her with a firm command and look, or by a gentle tap on her bottom. I could have also prevented the entire incident from occurring by placing her in her highchair, or a playpen. Given the growing hostility between her mother and I, I should have known that there would be no room for error.

After picking up the ticket at the police station, I began to realize not only the severity of being charged with child abuse, but also the lifelong ramifications of being convicted of such a charge. Having never been in "the system" and being completely oblivious to what was happening, I had no choice but to hire a defense attorney.

Lord, how could you allow this to happen to me, of all people? I have traveled to schools, churches, and juvenile detention centers encouraging kids and teenagers. I just got back from spending time at an orphanage in Haiti and I'm going to South Africa in a month to pour into the lives of more young people. Now I'm being charged with child abuse! Why?

A few days later, I realized this truth—the devil knows God created me for His divine purpose and he was trying to do everything he could to keep me from fulfilling that purpose. Therefore, despite the temptation to resent my daughter's mother for filing the child abuse against me—and believe me I was tempted—I asked God *to have mercy on her and not judge her*. I also asked God to help me love and forgive her, even through her effort to keep me from spending time with our daughter, just as God forgave me of my transgressions.

Prior to my daughter's birth, in January of 2010, while traveling around the country speaking to young people, encouraging them to make good choices, I heard from God, "I cannot fully use you because of all of the hatred and bitterness in your heart."

Hearing God's words, I fell to my knees, completely broken. My greatest desire was to become useful to God, but one thing had been standing in the way—my failure to relinquish my hatred toward my daughter's mother. Oddly enough, my hatred towards her had become a source of comfort to me. *As long as I live, I will hate her!* I often thought. In agony, I wept because I knew if I truly wanted to become *completely useful* to God, I had to rid myself of all the bitterness and hatred I harbored against her. In the midst of my jaded thinking, I forgot about the second greatest commandment Jesus gave us in chapter twenty-two of the book of Matthew, verse thirty-nine,

Love your neighbor as yourself (niv).

So with a sincere heart and a clear mind, I gave the Lord every ounce of hatred and bitterness I had stored up inside of me towards my daughter's mother. This was the first step God used in my process of forgiveness. Shortly after the day I gave up my anger and bitterness toward my daughter's mother, the Holy Spirit led me to read a book called *Led By Faith* about the life of Immaculée Ilibagiza—a Rwandan-born woman who survived the Rwandan genocide and her journey of forgiving the people who slaughtered her family. After reading the book, I thought, *If she can forgive the people who slaughtered and murdered her family, I have to be able to forgive my daughter's mother.*

So I forgave her—or so I thought.

One morning in July 2011, the Lord led me to the following scripture, where Jesus says to his disciples,

Take heed to yourselves: If your brother trespass against thee, rebuke him; and if he repent, forgive him. (Luke 17:3)

After reading this verse, the Holy Spirit gave me a deeper understanding of the process of forgiveness:

Step 1: The process of forgiveness cannot begin until I am willing to let go all of the anger, bitterness, and hatred I'm holding toward whoever has wronged me.

Step 2: I must confront the person who has wronged me—telling them out of love what they have done. If I have anger and hatred in my heart when I talk to them, it will only cause the situation to get worse, which is why I must complete step 1 first.

Step 3: After confronting the person, it is now up to them to acknowledge their wrongdoing and repent for wronging me.

Step 4: Only after a person repents can I fully forgive them. In 1John chapter one, verse nine, Paul says, "If we confess our sins, He is faithful and just to forgive us of our sins, and cleanse us from all unrighteousness." God cannot, and will not, forgive me unless I repent and confess my sins. Therefore, I cannot forgive others unless they repent. Simply put, there can be no forgiveness without repentance. Yet just as the Lord forgives whoever is willing to repent, so should I.

Step 5: Lastly, if the person is not willing to repent, I must say what Jesus said on the cross, "Father, forgive them for they know not what they do." Although Jesus forgave people of their sins while He walked on this earth (Luke 7:48), when he encountered people who were unrepentant (including myself at one time), he presented them before the Father, asking Him to deal with their unwillingness to repent.

As for the criminal charges I was facing, God allowed me to plead guilty to a lesser charge, and was sentenced to one year of probation. Why would I plead guilty? Well, after asking God, *Should I plead guilty to a lesser charge, or should I go to trial?*, while standing in the hallway of the courthouse, the Lord led me to chapter five of the book of Acts, where I found His answer to my question.

In this passage, Peter and those who were with him were brought before the high priest and the council of the elders because they were found teaching and preaching in the name of Jesus Christ. As they stood before the council, a Pharisee named Gamaliel stood and spoke in their defense, saying that if their preaching was of God, nothing would stand in its way—even the council itself. Hearing Gamaliel's words, the council decided to punish Peter and the Apostles by beating them, but then let them go free. In verse forty-one it states:

And they departed from the presence of the council, rejoicing that they were counted worthy to suffer shame for his name.

Why did Peter and the Apostles rejoice? They rejoiced because they believed it was better to obey the commission Jesus Christ had given them before He ascended to heaven, rather than obey man. The commission Christ gave those men is the same for all who believe in Him today. Jesus says, in the twenty-eighth chapter of the book of Matthew, verses 19-20,

Go ye therefore, and teach all the nations, baptizing them in the name of the Father, and of the Son, and of the Holy Ghost:

Teaching them to observe all things whatsoever I have commanded you: and lo, I am with you always, even unto the end of the world. Amen.

Like Peter and the Apostles, my action on the day of the incident involving my daughter was the result of my desire to obey God rather than man. In the thirteenth chapter of Proverbs, God teaches us what it means to discipline our children:

Those who spare the rod of discipline hate their children. Those who love their children care enough to discipline them (nlt).

I corrected my daughter out of my love for her, and my guilty plea was an admission of my choice to obey God rather than man. Therefore, just as Peter and the Apostles rejoiced, I too rejoice because I have been considered worthy to suffer for the sake of Christ.

What happened in my case was a small example of the devil's plan to turn the world against the way God has instructed parents to raise children. Prayer is no longer legal in public schools. If we reprimand our children, leaving a mark on their bodies, criminal charges will be brought against us. I can still recall my mother telling my brothers and me, "You can call the police on me if you want to, but I'm gon' beat you 'til they get here, and then I'm gon' beat you when I get back!" Hearing her words, my brothers and I never dared to call the police!

Now let me be perfectly clear—I DO NOT condone any form of child abuse. There has been, and continues to be, serious cases of child abuse today. However, if as a society we continue obeying man's laws and not God's, our children will surely suffer. More and more children will drop out of school, more children will run the risk of becoming addicted to drugs, teen pregnancy will increase, and ultimately more children will end up dead before they receive their high school diplomas.

God told me once, "Parents are in jeopardy of losing their parental rights. No, not their constitutional parental rights, but the parental rights I have given them! If parents do not begin praying for their children, laying their hands on them in an effort to ask for my protection over their lives, and begin teaching their children to value gifts from me more than any gift the world may offer them—they will cast their parental rights away. And guess who gets them when they toss them away? The devil."

In November 2010, I also decided to stop fighting and let God fight my battles for me. Following my sentencing in March 2011, I was scheduled to testify against my daughter's mother, which could have resulted in her being reprimanded by the court. But, the night before I was scheduled to testify against her in court, God told me to call my attorney and tell her to drop my claim against my daughter's mother—so I did. In that moment, a seed of longsuffering was planted inside me.

After hanging up the phone with my attorney, I fell to my knees and I wept out loud of sheer pain and agony, knowing this was a chance to see her experience some of the suffering I had endured. However, God revealed to me that my daughter was at an age where she feels every bit of pain her mother feels, and that any stone I would throw would cause more damage to her than her mother.

The last time I held my daughter in my arms was in a public library in November 2010. Since then, to prevent any other legal issues from arising, I have chosen to completely surrender my desire to be with my daughter to the Lord—a choice that is beginning to bare good fruit.

Despite all the stones her mother and I have thrown at each other—stones of blame, hatred and bitterness—upon entering the eleventh hour of my probation sentence in January 2012, and after nearly a year and a half of no communication between us at all—I received an email from my daughter's mother asking for my help as, understandably, Christmas caused her to get a little behind with bills. *God is giving me a chance to love her, as I love myself,* I thought. With that in mind, while containing my excitement, I sent her a warm reply and made plans to speak with her on the phone later that evening.

Thirty minutes later, after allowing the surprise of it all to sink in, I became consumed by a rollercoaster of emotions. I thought of the respect and regard I have always had throughout my entire life for single mothers—but in contrast, the amount of disrespect I had previously shown my daughter's mother. *I have been such a hypocrite,* I thought. The pain of my guilt and shame brought me to tears—and a seed of gentleness was planted inside me. Then, my tears of shame suddenly turned to tears of gratitude to God for giving me yet another chance to love my daughter's mother—as I love myself.

During the phone call later that evening, my daughter's mother shed tears as I asked her to forgive me for my trespasses against her. *The love of God truly transcends all boundaries and barriers.* Then she shared with me how our ever-so-amazing daughter, although somewhat shy, loves to play the guitar, sing, and play sports. She also sent me several recent photos of her. *God may have given her many of my talents and gifts, but, thankfully, He didn't give her my looks.* Before hanging up the phone, I asked for her banking information and stood in complete awe of how God used the money He has given me—the money that the devil had used to cause strife between us and to try to destroy our daughter—to open a door for, much needed, forgiveness and healing.

And if that wasn't enough, for the first time since November of 2010—in March of 2012, God allowed me to see and spend quality time with my daughter.

Today, as God allows my daughter's mother and I to cultivate a loving friendship—understanding that it will take tremendous work and effort on each of our part—I ask Him to teach me how to love her, as I love myself. I also ask God to teach me how to love my daughter, who is innocent of all wrongdoing and deserves all of my love and affection. My genuine belief is that one day her mother and I will be able to exhibit the love of Christ toward each other, and in doing so, set a wonderful example for our amazing *gift*.

Speaking of gifts, following a Sunday service, with a tender heart, I sat on the floor in my dining room as tears streamed down my face. One question came to my heart, "Lord, what constitutes a gift from you?"

God answered, "Anything you have received *as a gift* that you did not ask for, is a gift from me." After hearing His words, the stream of tears became a waterfall as I began to think of all the wonderful gifts God had given me—and all of my thoughts became centered on my little one. Not only did I not ask for my daughter, but also I regretfully gave her mother two thousand dollars to have her aborted. I dread the day that I will have to share this painful truth with her. Why will I tell her? Because she needs to know that her dad is far from perfect, and in spite of the love I have for her, she has a Father in heaven that loves her far more than I ever have—or ever will!

CHAPTER 11
UNEXPECTED ENCOUNTERS

My life has been filled with a series of strange events and unexpected encounters. Once I had purchased two tickets for my girlfriend and I to go to a theater performance in Denver. Before the evening arrived, she officially ended our relationship. I wondered who to take in her place. I finally chose to ask a woman with whom I had been casually involved with at the time. After she declined my offer, I heard a voice say, "I want to take you out on a date!"

In all of my years of wining and dining various women, it had never once occurred to me that the Lord wanted to spend quality time with me. When the night arrived for my "Date with Jesus," I put on my best and headed downtown.

When I arrived at the restaurant, the host asked, "For two?"

"Yes," I replied with a wide grin.

Once seated, I glanced at the couples surrounding me and I smiled confidently, as I was seated with the King of Kings Himself. After a peaceful dinner at one of my favorite restaurants, it was time to head across the street for the show. With two tickets in hand, I proudly walked up to the window, handed them to a female attendant and walked into the theater to take my seat. As I approached my seat I caught a glimpse of a woman who resembled my ex-girlfriend. My eyes were not deceiving me—it *was* my ex-girlfriend—on a date with another man. Confused and shocked, I thought, *Lord, what are you doing to me? You said you wanted to take me out on a date and then you allow her to be here with another guy?*

In an instant, my excitement turned to distress. And for a split second I contemplated leaving altogether. But I sucked it up and headed for my seat. As I passed my ex, the smile on her face was replaced by a puzzled and frustrated look when she saw me. She looked as if she had seen a ghost. Her friendly laughter ceased and I sensed a chill in the room—she did not look happy to see me. During the show I wondered, *Is this a sign that we are supposed to be together?* The following day, I went with my gut and purchased a second engagement ring. I gave it to her, asking her to reconsider our engagement. But after two weeks, she returned the ring, rejecting my attempt to reconcile.

Another of my chance encounters occurred in the beginning of 2011. This encounter involved a woman I met during a night out on the town back in 2008. The night we first met, a buddy of mine, who had been trying to get me out of the house for months, invited me to go out to a small bar near Denver. It didn't take long after stepping into the bar to remember why I stopped going to bars and nightclubs altogether. Surrounded by the thick smell of smoke and pressed against people attempting to drink away their sorrows, I began to question why I let my friend talk me into going out. That is, until I saw "her."

I was immediately captivated. Her eyes were brilliant and enchanting. Her skin was the color of honey, perfectly framed by her long-flowing, beautiful hair. I found myself slipping back into chase mode even though I had surrendered to Christ months ago. As I stood near the front door, she walked toward me heading for the exit. Our eyes locked, following each other's every move. I decided to chase.

By the time I made it outside she was already halfway up the flight of stairs to the street level.

"So you just gon' stare at me like that and not say anything?" I asked. She laughed as she made her way back down the stairs. We talked briefly. She made a comment that made me a little nervous, "My schedule is *really* crazy, so I don't know when we'll be able to catch up, but we'll see." *Not another stripper!* I thought. After exchanging phone numbers she left.

As we conversed well into the early hours of the morning later that night, I was relieved to learn she was not an exotic dancer. She was working on two graduate level degrees, hence the reason she had no time for a social life. During the two or three hours we spent on the phone that night, she earned a small measure of my trust, admitting that she was currently dating one of my former teammates and was currently working her way out of that relationship. We decided to hang out and get to know each other. All went well, until the night our friendship took the same wrong turn many others had before. Despite my newfound status with the Lord, my obsession with sex continued.

At the time I really didn't want to get emotionally or physically involved with anyone, since I knew it would interfere with my walk with Christ. Again, my spirit may have been willing, but my flesh was extremely weak. We decided it was best if we kept our involvement casual, realizing there were other people with whom each spent time. While that arrangement was nice in theory, we maintained a casual sexual relationship through the fall of 2010. Whenever we went extended periods of time without seeing each other we kept in touch, as we genuinely cared for each other. Then came the day that her life changed forever.

We had not seen each other for months, so we agreed to meet up at my house. It was the beginning of 2011 and the time she was supposed to be at my house came and went. I got worried and sent her a text message to make sure everything was all right. She responded back, "Hey, I'm sorry. I know I should have called you, but I am at the doctor's office right now. Nothing serious. Something came up unexpectedly and I have to deal with it right now."

"Call me," I texted out of my concern. Seconds later my phone rang.

"Hello."

"Hey, I'm really sorry but something came up that I have to deal with. It's nothing serious, so there's no need for you to worry."

"Okay, good," I responded. "So what's going on?"

"I'm two months pregnant." There was a moment of awkward silence as I let the words sink in. Speechless, my mind raced, trying to formulate some response.

"Oh. Well, I better let you go," I replied as I hung up the phone. A range of emotions flooded my mind. *Why didn't she tell me this two months ago?* On one hand, I felt relieved knowing I was not the father, as we had stopped having sex well before two months prior. On the other hand, I remembered the concerns she expressed during our involvement about my having a daughter with another woman. *Well, I wonder how she feels about me having a daughter with another woman now.* Honestly, I had felt deeply judged by her comments about me having a "baby mama." It was as if she were claiming innocence, while I was guilty of committing some horrible crime.

The whole discussion reminded me of a comment one of my former teammates made one day during a conversation in the locker room, "It's true Ian, and everybody knows I'm guilty of not using condoms, because I got two kids to prove it. But just because you don't have any kids to prove it, I know yo' a@@ don't use condoms!" He was right. I wrongly judged him and others for having children out of wedlock. Then I had a child out of wedlock. It was a hard lesson learned: don't judge others, because you just might find yourself judged the same way one day.

A week after she shared the news of her pregnancy, I decided to attend a late night movie with a group of friends. As we stood around, waiting for the last person to arrive, guess who walked into the theater—my newly pregnant friend with who I guessed was her child's father. Our eyes caught briefly and we exchanged a quick, "Hi" as she headed straight for the theater. Her and her child's father walked into the same movie my friends and I were going to watch.

During the movie it dawned on me, *Wait a minute, two of the main characters in this movie have our names. That's odd. Okay, Lord, what does this mean? Are you trying to send me some kind of sign? I mean what are the chances of her and I watching the same movie at the same time with two of the main characters sharing our names?*

After the movie, I noticed her child's father walking out of the entrance alone. I thought, *She must have gone to the bathroom and he went to get the car.* Then seconds later, I saw her walk out of the bathroom. We greeted each other with a half hug, spoke briefly, and parted ways. As I exited the theater, I smiled because it gave me peace to see her trying to make a relationship work with the father of her child, for their child's sake. Driving home, I remember thinking, *Lord, I'm not even going to try to figure out why that just happened. The last time something like this happened, I thought I was supposed to reconcile with my ex, which turned out to be wrong. This time I'll just wait for you to tell me why you allowed our paths to cross.* Regardless of the reason for our meeting, I was simply happy to see her with someone who appeared to be attentive and caring.

The next morning, God gave me insight into the encounter the night before. God revealed to me that encounters like the two described above, as well as the one with the exotic dancer from Florida who I encountered in Hong Kong, simply confirmed that I was right where He wanted me to be. Finally, I started to clearly see what God was revealing to me: I have wasted so much time analyzing and trying to figure out what each of my chance encounters had meant rather than seeing them for what they plainly were: a reminder that God is in control and has me right where He wants me. When I experience chance encounters today, I simply thank God for letting me know I am right where He wants me to be—and keep it moving!

Since my surrender to Christ, being in the right place at the right time has allowed me to cross paths with many wonderful people. Few, however, have had more impact on my life than a twenty-eight year old man I met while shopping for groceries. In 2010, as I pushed my cart toward the meat section in a local market, I crossed paths with a woman heading in the opposite direction down the aisle. Slowing down as I passed her, we shared a few words. As I turned toward her, I could sense a deep heaviness within her heart. This caused me to listen to her all the more attentively. During this brief pause, I noticed a young man standing near her. She introduced her son, Zac, and in an effort to acknowledge him, I extended my right hand. To my surprise, he took a few steps backward and placed his hands behind his back.

After apologizing, his mother said softly, "Oh no, it's okay. He has an illness." Before she could complete her sentence I immediately felt that God had brought us together. I looked at the young man a second time—this time I saw Zac in a different light. Minus the plastic gloves on his hands and his nervous energy, I saw his gentle spirit. With a look of both excitement and curiosity on his face, as the conversation with his mother came to a close I felt compelled to offer him something. Momentarily, the thought slipped away as I heard his mother's heart-felt response to my offer to pray for them, "Thanks. We'll take it. We need all the prayer we can get!"

After walking away, I continued thinking of him. *What am I supposed to offer him?* Minutes later our paths crossed for the second time, this time at the check out lane. After exchanging a few more words, we said our goodbyes and they walked away. As I watched them make their way toward the exit, I noticed Zac looking back at me. He walked out of the store with a huge smile on his face. It was at that moment I realized what I had to offer him, my *friendship*! But, it was too late to catch up with them. Walking out to my truck, I thought, *Okay Lord, if you allow me to see him again I will offer him my friendship.*

A month passed, and I entered the same market one day, much to my surprise, I saw Zac standing near the entrance. My spirit leaped for joy, as I knew God had given me a second opportunity to offer Zac my friendship. I didn't approach him abruptly, out of respect for his condition. Instead, I decided to wait until I saw him with his mother. Sure enough, I met them both standing in front of the very same place that we met the first time. After greeting them both, I gently asked his mother,

"You know, I was wondering if he has any friends?"

"No, he doesn't," she responded, "In fact, his best friend just passed away—his father."

My heart broke. It nearly burst out of my chest in its attempt to embrace Zac. I asked him if it would be okay for me to give his mother my contact information. "Sure," he said.

After giving his mother my phone number, she said, "You know what's interesting? He remembered you! He's even mentioned you a few times since the last time we saw you. He felt like there was something special about your spirit. In fact, when he saw you a few moments ago at the front of the store, he came and told me you were here!"

I was not at all surprised to hear this because I felt the same way. We went our separate ways and I thanked God for giving me a second chance. A week or so later, my phone rang. It was Zac calling. After learning a bit more about each other, I asked him if he would mind sharing the details about his illness. He explained, "I have allergic reactions to a number of chemicals used in perfumes, paints, and cleaning agents. Sometimes I experience psychological reactions as well." *So that explains the plastic gloves he had on in the grocery store*, I thought. During the course of our conversation he also shared how his emotional state fluctuated, as he grew more and more frustrated with his illness. We also talked about his brief history of friendships and I found out he was twenty-eight years old.

I thought, *He's twenty-eight and other than occasional visits to his grandmother's house and a grocery store trip, this illness has kept him bound to his house.* My heart ached for him. He shared his love for sports and how he loved to play basketball and watch football. He seemed to come alive when we started talking about sports! I sensed his genuine passion and love for them. We talked about me going over to his house and shooting hoops when the weather warmed up.

A few weeks later I drove over to his house and we played a few games of "horse" outside in his driveway. Following his victory, (he had home court advantage!) I needed a break, so I took a seat on a cement step and we talked a while. I learned that we shared the same faith in Christ, and I asked if he would pray with me. During our prayer, I thanked God for allowing our paths to cross, and I also asked Him to completely heal Zac from his condition. Following our prayer, I headed home full of peace and joy.

Days later, during a phone conversation, he told me that during our prayer he peeked out of the corner of his eye and saw a white dove flying to the top of a nearby evergreen tree. The Holy Spirit had been present during our moment of prayer.

Ten years ago, I would have seen no value in having a friendship with a twenty-eight year old virgin. However, today I am thankful to be able to say I realize the tremendous wealth and true significance his friendship offers. To this point in our lives, we both had longed for genuine friendship. I'm convinced that meeting each other the way we did, when we did, was nothing short of divine. There is so much I find amazing about how God has orchestrated our friendship. An appreciation for sports and our faith in Christ are obvious things we share, but other things we have in common didn't become obvious until we got to know each other more deeply—the feelings of loneliness and rejection, the desire to be loved and accepted. But the most amazing discovery I've made regarding our friendship is the one thing we don't have in common at all—while I've spent years chasing sexual relationships with numerous women, he's spent years searching and longing for the companionship of *one* woman.

Now, in addition to being thankful for each new person God allows me to cross paths with, I am also grateful for the confirmation God offers me through unexpected encounters with people from my past which signify that I am right where He wants me.

CHAPTER 12
THROUGH GOD'S EYES

Ever since the day the Lord told me I was *useless* to Him, I longed for the day He would tell me I had become *useful* to Him. In April 2009, traveling all over the country speaking into the lives of young people, at last God said, "Now you are useful to me." Hearing these words, if only for one moment, gave me reason to celebrate!

I didn't become useful to God because of all of the things I did—or stopped doing. Sure, I decided to no longer frequent nightclubs and strip clubs—but it was something more than that. There even came a day when it no longer gave me pleasure to use women for sex, as my new hope and desire for them was to see what God saw in them. Real change never happens quickly and I still remained sexually involved with a few women and continued to struggle with anger and bitterness. But I became *useful* to God because I finally allowed Him to use me for the purpose for which He created me.

Now, let me be clear, God does not *need* me! However, in chapter twenty-two of Matthew, verse fourteen, Jesus says,

> *For many are called, but few are chosen.*

You see, the Lord wouldn't have a reason to *choose us* if He didn't have a desire to *use us*. In fact, there are many examples of God using people for His divine purpose. God used Moses to lead the children of Israel out of Egypt. God used Noah to build the ark to save some from the flood. God used Paul to preach the gospel to the Gentiles. God used His only begotten Son, Jesus, to take away the sin of the world. And yes, God, even wanted to use me for His divine purpose—but I had to allow Him to do so. When I finally chose to surrender to Him, He began to use me in ways that I could have never dreamed. Traveling across the country and beyond spreading the gospel, caring for orphans and widows, and helping those in poverty are just a few of the ways I began to see God using me when I allowed Him to.

As I entered 2010 with a growing desire to see *through God's eyes* and become even more useful to Him, He said, "Last year, I took you from state to state—this year I am going to take you from country to country!" At the time, I didn't know how, when, or where God would make it all happen, but I was determined to be ready when He said go. So, with great anticipation, I waited for Him to reveal what country He would send me to first.

After a month or so of waiting, I began hearing about the devastation caused in Haiti by the massive earthquake. Recalling the prophetic word from God I received from another one of my cousin Darrian's close friends a year earlier,

I began to wonder—*Lord, is this where you want me to go?* Here is a portion of that prophetic word, which I received in the spring of 2008:

> *There is something about restoration—both in the spiritual and in the natural—that is going to play a major component in your life. The Lord is going to send you to places where destruction has occurred. I also see that there is going to be authority that is going to come upon you in these latter days—I see you literally standing in the middle of what looks like a "bombed out city." You have this look of ABSOLUTE DETERMINATION and CONFIDENCE in the Lord to bring about His purposes—even in the midst of such disaster. It seems almost as if you are right at home. It is powerful! I can sense the authority that is going to rest upon you even as I see you in this vision. You won't back down. When disaster strikes, you will be one equipped by the Lord to bring about a swift and complete restoration.*

After reading this message again, I prayed—*Lord, if you want me to go to Haiti you will have to make it all happen*—and so He did. I was asked to visit an orphanage in Haiti just a few months later! Before leaving, the Lord gave me a revelation, which I would get to see with my own eyes during my visit. In chapter seven of the book of John, verses 40-44, it states:

> *Many of the people therefore, when they heard this saying, said, Of a truth this is the Prophet. Others said, This is the Christ. But some said, Shall Christ come out of Galilee? Hath not the scripture said, That Christ cometh of the seed of David and out of the town of Bethlehem, where David was? So there was a division among the people because of him. And some of them would have taken him; but no man laid hands on him.*

After reading this passage, God said, "There were people who did not believe Jesus was the Son of God simply because He was from *Galilee*—a place deemed worthless by many. Ian, any person, place, or material item in your life that you treat like Galilee, STOP! For the very person, place, or item which you, or the world deems worthless or useless is exactly what—or whom—I will use for my divine purposes!" I immediately began examining my life for people, places, or material items I had deemed worthless. After my time of reflection, I confessed and repented to God. As the days passed, the Lord gave me an even greater understanding of "Galilee"—that Galilee was a place of hidden treasures. One day God led me to chapter two of the book of Matthew, verses 19-22:

> *But when Herod was dead, behold, an angel of the Lord appeareth in a dream to Joseph in Egypt,*

Saying, Arise and take the young child and his mother and go into the land of Israel: for they are dead which sought the young child's life.

And he arose and took the young child and his mother and came into the land of Israel.

But when he heard that Archelaus did reign in Judaea in the room of his father Herod, he was afraid to go thither: notwithstanding, being warned of God in a dream, he turned aside into the parts of Galilee.

Not only does Galilee symbolize what and whom God uses for His own divine purposes, but also, as we see from the passage above, God warned Joseph in a dream to take his wife Mary and baby Jesus into Galilee—making Galilee the very place where He hides that which is most precious to Him!

When I arrived in Haiti, the revelation I received concerning Galilee became visible to me. There amidst the death, disaster and destruction of the earthquake, I stood in total awe of the beauty, strength, and resilience of the beautiful Haitian people. I spent an entire week at an orphanage—a first for me! During my years in the NFL, I was only concerned with chasing women and my next purchase. I never took time to stop and think of the millions of children around the world who did not have parents, who did not have anyone to teach him or her how to pray, to sing them to sleep at night, or teach them how to kick, throw, and catch a ball.

During my first night, I met my roommate, a South African born pastor who lives in the States. He told me, "Hey, brother, I know we just met and I don't know what you have going on in July and August later this year, but there's a program I'll be running in South Africa, and I just feel led to invite you to come and be a part of what God is doing there."

Humbled by his invitation and, remembering that God said he would be taking me from country to country, I replied, "Thank you for the invitation. I will submit it to the Lord in prayer and get back to you when I receive an answer from Him."

I stood in complete amazement as I watched God bring to pass His promise! In the twenty-third chapter of the book of Numbers, verse nineteen, Balaam says,

God is not a man that he should lie; neither the son of man that he should repent: hath he said and shall he not do it? or hath he spoken and shall he not make it good?

When God gives His word, we can always count on Him keeping it!

Looking back at my stay at the orphanage in Haiti, there are many moments that stand out and resonate in my heart and mind. There is one in particular, however, which stands out more than the others—one I hope to reflect upon for the rest of my life and one-day share with my children and grandchildren. The moment is best described in my following journal entry:

There are no movie theaters, no game consoles, no shopping malls, or amusement parks here to keep kids preoccupied and entertained. Instead children of all ages take pleasure in the simplest things in life—drawing with crayons on a sheet of paper, making friendship bracelets, being recorded on video along with ten other children, and then watching it on the tiny camera display. I have observed and witnessed so much during my short visit to Haiti; however, tonight is simply the icing on the cake! There are approximately one hundred children here at the orphanage and as the sun began to set, the clouds began to close in, and the rain started to fall, I noticed the children were still playing and laughing. So, being a big kid myself, I joined them! We all formed a human train and spent about fifteen or twenty minutes running and bouncing around the compound singing songs and chanting in Haitian Creole, "Kat de taw de set! Kat de twa de set!"—Which they began chanting after the soccer game we played earlier in the day.

I have to say it was the greatest time I have ever spent playing in the rain! Seeing the smiles on the children's faces and hearing them sing praises to the Lord in their native tongue was healing for my soul. In that moment I truly found myself in the center of "Galilee." These are orphans who, according to the world, have nothing to be cheerful about. They should be sulking in their miserable circumstances, but no! Each of these children represents one of God's most precious gifts! Although the world may not see value in their lives, God is sure to do a wonderful and marvelous work through the orphans of Haiti!

Finally, after we all grew tired from the fun of parading around the village—running, jumping, singing, and chanting our hearts out—the children all went to their dormitories and I made my way up onto the rooftop. As I looked out over the compound, one thing became clear. Regardless of our circumstances, we all have the power to make the best of what we have—even if it's rain falling from the sky in Haiti.

I was exhausted when the time for me to leave finally arrived! After being a human jungle gym for an entire week, going without a shower, and being away from my daughter, I looked forward to my return home! Little did I know, however, in the coming months I would be departing for another journey!

A week or so following my return from Haiti, God gave me the green light to accompany the pastor to South Africa! So, in July 2010, right after receiving the citation for child abuse and the day after Papa passed away, I set out for the "Mother Land" with a heavy heart. I was confident that God was sending me to South Africa for His divine purpose, so I had no other choice than to do what God instructed me to do—plus I knew my grandfather would have wanted me to go.

Before my departure to South Africa, I received another revelation—this time it concerned the word "go." What I learned was this: Those who are willing to "go" and "let go" when God tells them to will surely be blessed and rewarded because God is faithful to reward those who are obedient to His instructions.

One day, I received an unexpected phone call from my cousin Nathaniel who I had not spoken to since collecting grass stains on my dress clothes as a child. While we were on the phone, he asked, "Hey, cuz, I'm relocating my family to Nevada in the next month or so. I am going out early to finalize a few details and will be driving through Colorado tonight. Would it be okay if I stop over and get some rest at your place?"

"Of course," I replied.

Following his arrival, we immediately began to share all that God had been doing in each of our lives since we had last seen each other. After listening to his testimony, I shared how God had allowed me to spend all of 2009 traveling around the country sharing my life experiences with young people. As I began sharing with him the list of all of the different places I visited, he began to chuckle.

"What? What's so funny?" I asked.

"No, I am not laughing at you," he said. "My pastor once said, 'The blessing is in the GO.' And if you went to all of the places God told you to go to last year, you have a lot of blessings coming your way!"

After receiving his words of encouragement, I became excited as I reflected on each and every place God had sent me over the course of the previous twelve months. I specifically remember visiting a grade school in New York. Full of excitement and anticipation, I arrived at the school, but I found myself frustrated and annoyed after speaking to the head administrator. The school wide assembly I had originally planned to participate in had somehow been changed to individual classroom visits! *Huh? You want me to visit how many classrooms?* I reminded myself that God sent me there for His divine purpose and to be useful to Him. I quickly got over it. After visiting about ten classrooms, by the end of the day, not only did I sound like a CD stuck on repeat, I was exhausted!

But, after hearing and receiving what my cousin Nathaniel had just shared with me, I realized that even though I was reluctant and frustrated, God was pleased with me because of my willingness to "go." This wisdom stuck with me, challenging me to look beyond the appearance of the opportunities and instead focus on being useful to God. I gladly carried this new wisdom with me to South Africa.

Upon my arrival to South Africa, I immediately started making new friends, which included about fifty high school students from the US, oddly enough. I met many wonderful people from countries all over the continent of Africa—

Zambia, Zimbabwe, and Mozambique, just to name a few, as well as a host of South African natives. During my stay, I traveled all across the country—from west to east, and north to south. As I look back on my time in South Africa, there were so many wonderful blessings that came out of my trip! While at a school one day, a young boy who had been very quiet in class and his cousin followed me out to my van. He wore a sad expression as he handed me a piece of paper with a name written on it.

"Hello there," I said. "Whose name is this?"

"My mother's," he replied. "Can you pray for her?"

He risked being made fun of and ridiculed by his classmates for the sake of his mother, I thought. I gently placed my hand on his shoulder.

"Yes, can I pray for her now?"

As his eyes swelled with tears, he and his cousin both nodded their heads. By the time I finished praying for him and his mother, a bright smile found a home on his precious face! Following our prayer, I began to understand more deeply why the Lord sent me across the Atlantic Ocean—God wanted me to pour out on these South African children all the love He had been showering on me over the course of my life.

Another moment that still resonates in my heart occurred one Sunday morning in service. As I stood in the sanctuary witnessing the African people praising and worshipping the Lord, I began to weep uncontrollably. I tried to make myself stop crying, but I couldn't stop the tears from flowing. Eventually I fell to my knees and wept like a baby. It felt as if the very place I stood and knelt upon was holy ground. Looking out over all of the beautiful African faces, I could see my mother, brothers, Grandma and Papa, and members of my extended family worshiping the Lord with all of our African ancestors through African dance and song. It felt as if I had not only been reunited with my past, but also with something deep inside me. I yearned to praise and worship God without inhibition, just as I witnessed my African brothers and sisters doing. By the end of service, I felt emotionally drained and overwhelmed, almost to the point of exhaustion.

Afterwards, I made the short walk back to the five-bedroom, non-hot water "man cave" which twenty-two of us men volunteered to lodge in. While walking, I began asking God—*Why me? Why did you choose me, of all people, to make this journey?*

What I found puzzling was why God would have me—of all people—travel such a great distance to speak to young people about abstinence and AIDS. I had been the last person to have *ever* practiced abstinence. In fact, there were even a few women I was sexually involved with in the weeks and months leading up to my departure to South Africa. But in the months following my return, I would learn why the trip was inevitable.

I had the pleasure of meeting an extremely gifted and talented eleven-year-old boy during my travels through South

Africa and on the first I met him, I learned that this young orphan was the fastest, strongest, and brightest boy in the group. I also learned that he was HIV positive. The news of his illness was heartbreaking, but there was still a sense of aliveness to him!

One night, as we all prepared for bed, I noticed him pull a notebook out of his bag. "What's that?" I asked.

"My journal."

"You have a journal?"

"Yes, I love to write."

His passion for writing made me grow even fonder of him. He reminded me so much of myself as a young boy, it was almost surreal. Perhaps this is why I wasn't surprised when I was asked to look after him during our stay at the camp. He had to take medication for his illness at seven o'clock in the morning and seven o'clock in the evening—not a minute sooner or later! I felt honored to be asked to look after and care for him, and happily took him under my wing!

At one point I began to think—*I wonder how he feels? I mean not having parents is one thing, but he has HIV on top of that!* I didn't know it at the time, but God was about to show me a glimpse of his troubled heart.

During a teambuilding exercise, we were shown a table with some random items on it. When the facilitators asked for someone to make up a fictitious story using the items, I thought—*I know just who to ask!* Making eye contact with the young boy, I asked him to create a story using his imagination. He shook his head—*No way!* After asking a few of the other children and receiving similar responses, I got the young boy's attention again—*Come on, be a leader!* I suggested.

Finally, after a few seconds of silence, he agreed to make up a story. As he began to share his story with the group, one of the young girls giggled. The minute he heard the giggle he stopped and immediately became very upset. "See! I knew this would happen."

We all stood in silence and I noticed a single tear trickle down his face. *I see your pain.* I could see him battling the same feelings of rejection, loneliness, frustration, and anger I battled at his age. I walked over to him. Resting my arm around his shoulder, I asked him to take a short walk with me. During our short time away from the others, God gave me an amazing opportunity to share with him what I battled against throughout my childhood and adolescent years. Having the ability to share with him was healing for my soul and I realized something very important—God allowed me to experience rejection, loneliness, and anger as a child so I could help children who felt the same. Therefore, I look forward to many more opportunities to encourage people who are plagued with feelings of loneliness, rejection, and anger.

Upon returning from South Africa, I shared about my encounter with the young boy with HIV with my mother during a phone conversation one evening. She made an interesting observation, "Ian, here you were, on another continent, and God assigned *you* to look after and care for a young boy who, though full of life, parentless, and not even thinking about sex, contracted HIV. He wasn't out committing senseless and foolish actions, yet still each day he has to deal with all of the ridicule, persecution, and unwarranted judgment that comes with the disease."

I began thinking of all the senseless sexual encounters I had experienced during the course of my life. "Mom," I said reluctantly, "it should've been me." My heart sank as I continued, "Despite all the women I've had sex with, God protected me from contracting any life-threatening and incurable diseases. But, this poor child is suffering. It just doesn't seem fair."

I experienced another profound moment in South Africa while sitting in the sanctuary where we held our daily meetings in Lusikisiki—a small rural town in the Transvaal area. As I sat conversing with a group of teenagers, the pastor of the church, Pastor Martin Mwape, interrupted the conversation and asked, "Excuse me brother, but do you mind if I have a word with you?"

"No," I replied, as I stood to my feet. "I don't mind at all."

"Since the time I saw you in service on Sunday morning, I have not been able to get your face out of my mind."

"Okay," I said.

"I would like to pray for you if you will allow me to. But first I must tell you that the Lord has given me a word for you. It is Mark 1:17—Jesus says, *'Come ye after me and I will make you to become fishers of men.'* You see, God revealed to me that He is doing something new with you, which is why people do not understand you or many of the recent decisions you have made in your life."

"Thank you for the word, Pastor, and I receive it," I responded.

"Okay, can I pray with you now?"

"Absolutely," I said as I slid from my chair to my knees before him, "Please."

This moment of prayer was only the second time in my entire life I humbled myself before a man. As I knelt before him, he began proclaiming the word he had spoken over my life. At the completion of his prayer, I thanked him and we embraced.

After our time of prayer, I sat alone in the sanctuary astonished and in awe of God. *Lord, you brought me all the way to South Africa to receive this word and impartation from a man of God—a true "fisher of men."* I began flooding God with question after question regarding what it meant to be a fisher of men. In all of my questioning, God revealed a great deal to me. One specific nugget of wisdom God gave me pertained to a question I asked God prior to my surrender to Christ—*How could Jesus Christ live on this earth and willingly suffer all of the persecution, ridicule, physical abuse, and punishment and never judge or condemn one single person?*

God's answer was, "Jesus was able to suffer because he saw each and every person—murderers, adulterers, sick, healthy, good, evil, rich, or poor—simply as *fish*. In the sea, there are many types of fish—some large, some small, fish that kill and eat other fish, and fish that eat seaweed and other forms of plant life. Some fish are considered dirty or unhealthy to eat because they are bottom feeders. There are other fish that, due to their rarity, are considered a delicacy. All in all, however, they are *all* fish! So when Jesus looked at a blind beggar, a young rich ruler, a murderer, an adulterer, or even those who persecuted him—he simply saw a fish that his Father sent him to save."

Since hearing these words, instead of seeing people as the world sees them—liars, celebrities, thieves, murderers, VIPs, backstabbers, do-gooders, or evildoers—I try to see people as simply fish that Christ desires to catch.

As my three-week journey through South Africa neared its end, during my last night in Lusikisiki, one of the young African men shared his deep-hearted fears and concerns. Standing before the entire group, he lamented, "You all are going back to America tomorrow, but I will still be here. I have nothing to offer these people. The children are hungry, but I have no food to give them. The people have needs, but I have nothing to give. I just don't know how I can help these people. Please pray for me because I am discouraged."

Sensing the despair within his heart, I said a short prayer. *Lord, please give me a word of encouragement to share with him right now.* Just then, God reminded me of something He had taught me a year prior—that "obedience is better than sacrifice." Ever since my childhood, I heard many people refer to the following scripture in the fifteenth chapter of first Samuel, verse twenty-two:

> *And Samuel said, 'Hath the LORD as great delight in burnt offerings and sacrifices, as in obeying the voice of the LORD? Behold, to obey is better than sacrifice . . . '"*

Hearing this scripture many times before, I never truly understood it's meaning until I asked God. He gave me an answer, "If I gave you a million dollars and told you to go sacrifice it, in Biblical times it would have literally meant to physically place the money on an altar and burn it up. And because the money would have been burned to ashes, there could have been no increase from it. But instead of telling you to sacrifice the million dollars, I told you to sow, or invest, some of the money here and invest some of the money there—if you are *obedient* in doing what I instruct you to do, I will be able to bring forth increase and multiply the money that you have sown!"

After receiving God's words, I sat speechless. It finally made sense! *Whatever God gives to me, I am responsible to do*

Plant Water Grow

whatever He instructs me to do with it. Some of the gifts God had given me in the past I have taken for granted—time, money, friendship, and love. After learning this truth, I finally recognized where I went wrong. God didn't say, "Ian, go waste and squander all of your time, money, and energy chasing women and hanging out in strip clubs, nightclubs, and casinos." Rather, God wanted me to use all of the gifts and resources He had given me for His divine purposes. But as a result of my *disobedience*, God could not—and did not—bring forth any increase from all of the time, money, and energy I wasted over the years.

After listening to the young man's heartfelt concerns, and being prompted by the Holy Spirit, I was compelled to share with him the value of his *obedience*. I said,

> *Although you feel like you have nothing to give or offer the people of Lusikisiki—you do. What you have is far more valuable than any amount of money or material gifts you could ever offer—your obedience to God. Your willingness to do whatever God instructs you to do for the people of Lusikisiki—whether that is to teach children in schools, share the gospel with people who have never heard it, or give someone the shirt off of your back—the reality is, God can and will bring forth increase from your obedience.*

As I spoke, I knew the Holy Spirit was speaking through me. Hearing my own words enlightened and ministered to me.

Unfortunately my disobedience continued after I returned home. I remained sexually active with three women, one of whom I actually met while she and her co-workers cleaned my home. The day I worked up the nerve to ask for her phone number, another woman was at my house, someone I had been in a sexual relationship with since the spring of 2010. While the other woman and I talked, I took notice of the cleaning lady. Although she spoke very little English, I needed no translator to communicate my desire to be intimate with her. After watching her work, I finally made my move by discreetly giving her my phone number as she left.

A few days later, she called and we met at a popular Mexican restaurant for our one and only dinner date. From that point on, we ordered take out or delivery to conceal our sexual indiscretion. Over the course of the next few months, we repeated the cycle—she would come over after she got off work, we would have sex, and I would order dinner.

Our sexual relationship came to an end in October 2010 and is, with the help of the Lord, going to be my last sexual relationship until God allows me to take a woman's hand in marriage.

I never imagined throughout my collegiate and NFL years that one day I would be able to say that I have been abstinent for over a year, let alone a week. But finally, after nearly four years of living surrendered to Christ, God is causing a seed of faithfulness to grow inside me. As my faithfulness to God increases, roots from the seed of self-control planted within me, are finally destroying my once paralyzing desire to chase women. Though this is by far the longest period of time I have ever gone without having sex since I began at age seventeen, I take none of the credit. God is the one who has worked in me both to will and to do His good pleasure (Philippians 2:13).

In the months following my last sexual relationship, God gave me more insight as to why obedience is better than sacrifice. God said, "There have been a number of women you have met who you knew you were not supposed to pursue. Out of your lustful desires, you were disobedient and became sexually involved with them anyway. What you've failed to realize is that I was the one who eventually caused those relationships to end, which resulted in the pain and suffering you and the women experienced. Had you been obedient from the beginning and not pursued them, no one would have suffered."

Reflecting back over the years, I took inventory of the relationships that caused me to suffer due to my unwillingness to resist the temptation to chase. Whether it was a one-night stand or a seven-year relationship, I caused, as well as endured, emotional pain and suffering that could have been prevented had I never become sexually involved with those women.

A few months prior to my becoming abstinent, God began teaching me some much-needed lessons regarding the *true value of women.* In the middle of service one Sunday morning, I caught a glimpse of someone walking down the aisle. As I turned to look, I noticed a woman standing in the isle. Acknowledging her beauty, I looked up to the Lord and thought—*Lord, she is absolutely beautiful, but all I want is more of you.*

Following service, I greeted a few of my friends and then exited the building. One thought stuck in my head: *This is strange. If the "old Ian" had seen her, he would've immediately switched gears and began to chase.* Letting that thought fully sink in, I recognized that the shift that had occurred in my spirit in April 2008 had finally begun to occur in my flesh—body and mind. The much-needed shift in my response and behavior towards beautiful women that I had desperately been seeking was finally manifesting itself in my life.

I felt weird, but great, all at the same time! Although I had been praying and asking the Lord to take away my desire to chase women, for Him to finally answer my prayer *was an absolute miracle!* After the service on the following Sunday, I decided to go out to lunch with a group of people—and the beautiful woman I noticed the previous Sunday happened to be there as well. As I sat and listened to her conversation, I found that, along with her beauty, she also had quite an intellect. *With her background in marketing, maybe we can discuss the projects I am currently working on over lunch.* So I asked her for her contact information.

A few days later, we agreed to meet for lunch. During lunch, I learned she was also the captain of her college rugby team. *She loves the Lord, she's a model, an intellectual, AND has the heart of a lioness!* I thought. While her entire being beamed with natural beauty, I didn't find myself needing to have her as I did with so many other beautiful women before. I felt puzzled.

Climbing into bed later that evening, I asked God why I was not attracted to her like I had been with other women. His answer floored me. "You are not *attracted* to her, because you are *in awe* of her. In the same way that Adam, being in awe, gazed upon all of my beautiful and wonderful creations in the Garden of Eden, you gaze at her because you are in awe of not only how wonderfully I created her, but *who it was* that created her."

This understanding completely blew me away! For the first time in my life, God revealed to me the difference between being "attracted" to a woman and being "in awe" of a woman. My attraction to a woman was selfishly based on what I liked—curves, long beautiful hair and sex appeal. The truth is, however, that being in awe of a woman has nothing to do with what I like at all. To be in awe of a woman, I first had to be in awe of the God who created her; then, and only then, could I be in awe of how wonderfully and beautifully He created her. This new understanding became the starting point for a whole new understanding of the *true value of women*.

God also began sharing with me the *true value of a wife*. One day, God said to me, "When and if I allow you to take a woman's hand in marriage, you will do so not because you simply want her to be the mother of your children or want to grow old and gray with her. You will only enter into marriage when you are able to look at her and say, 'I want to spend the rest of my life doing the Lord's work with you.' Every other reason to marry is secondary to this."

And a few months later, God said, "First I created the heavens, then I created the earth and everything therein. I created Adam and the Garden of Eden, and placed Adam in the Garden. Finally—*hear me when I say this*—before I rested on the seventh day I created Eve and gave her to Adam as a gift! Now, I could have waited until *after* I rested on the seventh day, or even *two thousand years after* the day I rested to create Eve, but I didn't! May this cause you to understand how much I value the gift of a wife."

Although the Lord used my mother, at times, to remind me that I should honor and treat women with the utmost respect, there was never a man in my life who took the time to teach me the true value of a woman—or wife. Now that God is teaching me about it, I am finally beginning to understand why it is important to honor and respect all women—*through God's eyes* they have all been fearfully and wonderfully made.

CHAPTER 13
TODAY

The rejection and loneliness I experienced when I was a little boy eventually led to my having little faith in people as an adult. My trust issues were not confined to women alone, of course—you can imagine the issues I have had with trusting men. In fact, I can count on one hand how many of my former teammates I allowed into my home during my eight-year professional career. While it has always been extremely difficult for me to trust people, while playing for the Denver Broncos an incident occurred that, ultimately, caused me to keep my guard up at all times.

When I first arrived in Denver, I truly thought people working within the Broncos organization were looking out for my best interest. That is, until I blew out the anterior cruciate ligament (ACL) of my knee in October 2004. I remember the circumstances leading up to my injury as if they happened yesterday. When I entered the fourth and final year of my rookie contract, I naturally expected to be financially rewarded for all of my hard work over the previous years. With the start of the regular season nearing, and understanding that I would be risking getting injured each time I stepped out on the football field, I became more focused on contract negotiations than on playing football.

At the time, my agent communicated my desire to negotiate a new contract, but the front office only responded, "Well, we just want to wait and see how things pan out this season before we enter negotiations." Translation: "Um, we want to wait to see if you get injured this season, because if you do get injured, we'll be able to sign you to a new deal for a discounted price."

Hearing the team's stance, I immediately thought—*I just went to my first Pro Bowl. I've played through injuries and pain and this is the appreciation and thanks I get! Where is their loyalty? Where is their appreciation for all of my hard work and effort?* I would soon learn the organization had no allegiance to its players.

With the frustrations of my contract constantly on my mind, I didn't want to play at all. But I had no choice in the matter, so I continued to work my butt off, starting off the season extremely well on the field. After the fifth game of the season, however, I had reached the limit of my patience. So I prayed, *Lord, if there is any way for me to finish the rest of the season without playing and still receive my paycheck, then please let it happen!* I meant every word.

During the next game, while running down the field to cover a punt, I planted my right foot in order to stop. My knee gave out, and I immediately fell to the ground. I felt a sharp pain in my right knee as I rolled around on the ground.

I got up and walked off the field without the assistance of my athletic trainers, but I noticed a looseness in my knee that I didn't feel previously. With only minutes before halftime, my concerns prompted me to head straight for the locker room. Taking a seat on the examination table, several of the doctors who followed me examined my knee.

"I think there's a fifty percent chance of his ACL being torn," I heard one of the doctors whisper to the others. And then, moments later, much to my surprise, one of the assistant trainers came over and said, "Okay, this is the plan—we're gonna ice it for a little while, then we want you to try to go back out and give it a go in the third quarter."

"Are you f@*!ing kidding me?" I roared, sitting up on the table. "I just heard doc say he thinks it's fifty percent torn! And now you think I'm 'bout to go back out there and 'give it a go?' You must think I'm stupid! I want my knee scanned *now*!"

With a perplexed and dazed look on his face, the trainer walked away. A few minutes later he returned. "Ian, unfortunately, we can't get your knee scanned until tomorrow morning, because there are no technicians available on Sunday."

"So you mean to tell me I work for a billion dollar organization that can't find someone to do a scan on my knee? Okay then, let me tell you what I'm 'bout to do. I'm goin' to get my a@@ in the shower, put my clothes on, and then I'm goin' to the closest emergency room I can find and have them scan my mutha f@!*in' knee! And don't worry, I'll be sure to tell the media about how I was treated after the game!"

With that, I hopped off of the table and walked into the locker room. I removed my uniform and pads and hit the shower. Then, just as I exited the shower, the assistant trainer came up to me. "Okay Ian, we were able to find a technician and she'll meet you up at the clinic right now, so get dressed and we'll have someone take you over there."

Absolutely amazing! I had to threaten to tell the media just to get a knee scan! I thought, shaking my head. After getting dressed I left the stadium. Following the scan, I asked the technician for her diagnosis.

"Yeah, your ACL is torn. I'm sorry. You can see it right there," she said pointing to the film.

On one hand, I felt relieved to hear the news. On the other hand, I was pissed! *They intentionally wanted me to go back out on the field so I could cause even more damage to my knee.* I was outraged!

In the weeks and months that followed, several individuals in the front office assured me I would receive a new contract. "Yeah," one said, "we're still gonna give you a new contract."

Right! They did offer me a new contract following the season, but the only problem was the amount of their offer—it was a joke. So, having faith my market value would increase once I proved my knee was fully recovered, I respectfully declined their offer. On the open market, following a few visits with different teams, I made a decision to take my services to Tampa, Florida.

So in 2005, with a *huge* chip on my shoulder—and an understanding that the only concern the people in the front offices had was ensuring that their own job was secure—I headed to Tampa. And as you can imagine, it didn't take long for the coaching staff in Tampa to witness the effects of my increased lack of trust. I went from a player who was willing to "take one for the team"—to a complete asshole, as one of my teammates labeled me one day as we laughed and joked. I had very little trust and respect for anyone—it didn't matter who they were, or what titles they held, if I felt they weren't genuine I didn't hesitate to let them know what I thought!

There were several incidents in which I took out my frustration and lack of trust on the coaches, and even the owners. Following one of our five wins that season, the owner of the Buccaneers walked through the locker room. When he finally made his way to me, standing there butt naked, I refused to shake his hand and turned my back to him. He only came into the locker room after wins and that pissed me off! As the owner walked away, one of my teammates said, "Ian, really? You're not gonna shake the man's hand?"

"Nope!" I replied, "His a@@ don't come shake my hand after we lose a game, so don't come shake my hand after we win!"

As my year in Tampa progressed, I dealt with my issues in the same way I always had—sleeping with women. Sex became the answer to all of my worries. If coaches pissed me off, I would go hang out at a strip club to find a girl to have sex with. With a brand new stable of women to choose from and my girlfriend still back in Denver, there was no need for discretion. It didn't matter if I was angry, lonely, happy, or sad—sex was my upper and downer. Immediately following my surrender to Christ, however, my thinking began to change—and thankfully so did my attitude toward life and people as well. When I would see former teammates or players, I would ask, "So, where you headed?"

"Oh! I'm headed to Vegas," or "I'm headed down to the islands," or "I'm headed down to Miami," they often responded.

"No!" I'd say, "To *heaven* or *hell*?"

Their responses to my question varied—some would immediately avoid eye contact, others would respond out of apprehension and uncertainty—"Uh, heaven," or "Yeah, man, I'm workin' on that."

The best response I ever heard, however, was from my younger cousin, Greg. I called him up one day and asked, "What up, boy! Where you headed?"

"I'm, uh…wait…hold up…it depends on what you mean," he said.

"Heaven or hell?" I replied—with a big smile on my face.

"Oh! I'm headed to heaven!" he replied confidently. "And if you would've called me three minutes ago, I would've been headed to heaven then, too!"

We both laughed. Following our conversation, I hung up the phone feeling a sense of joy and pride. In fact, after witnessing him win his first Super Bowl in February 2011 as a member of the Green Bay Packers, the same feeling of joy and pride immediately returned. Greg was the first player interviewed immediately following the game. The reporter asked him about the victory and *my spirit leaped for joy* when I heard him say, "To God be the glory!" His proclamation, even if for only three seconds, turned the attention and focus of nearly one hundred million people to God!

In 2010, God finally revealed to me a way to cope with feelings of anger and frustration, which did not involve having sex with multiple women. Following an extremely stressful morning, I found myself getting very upset and agitated about something that had just happened. I talked to my mother about the incident, and then my oldest brother, Jason, called me. Tears began to fall down my face and a rage rose up from deep inside of me as I drove down the freeway. I began to shout and curse at the top of my lungs, while my big brother quietly listened on the other end of the phone line.

Once I became somewhat settled down, Jason—who is now a devoted husband, loving father, respected mentor, police officer and, one of my closest friends—began to offer me encouragement. After listening for a while, I thanked him and hung up. Despite hearing my brother's words, I continued to cry out to the Lord the rest of the way home in an effort to release all of my frustration and anger.

Then finally, when I pulled up to my house, God said, "From now on, whenever you get angry or frustrated, bring your anger to me—I am big enough to handle it!" Hearing this, I felt a calm in the midst of my storm. There had never been anyone in my life that was able to calm me when I got angry or frustrated—so God became the first. While my mother and brothers had always been there for me to talk to, when I felt a need to let out my anger in a more expressive manner, I would often excuse myself from their presence or get off of the phone out of respect for them—I felt that raising my voice was disrespectful to them. So when God spoke to me about letting out my anger to Him, I felt relieved. *I don't have to suppress or store up my anger and frustration any more.*

Today, when I get angry or frustrated, God calms me in the same way Jesus calmed the storm, by rebuking the wind and speaking to the sea (Mark 4:39). There are also times now I find myself shouting to God at the top of my lungs—out of joy, excitement, and even love—because now I know He's big enough to handle *all* of my emotions!

As I look back over my entire journey, I see the patience of Jesus Christ and how far and deep His love traveled to save me. In spite of the rejection and loneliness I felt as a child and the unwise decisions I made over the past fifteen years of my life, by *faith* I believe that the blood of Jesus Christ has completely washed away all of my wrongdoing.

Speaking of faith, I never lacked confidence or faith while I was growing up! I had the faith as a thirteen year old to make the sixth grade football team, which gave me the faith to make the seventh, eighth, and the ninth grade teams. In other words, my faith increased with my age. And just as my faith increased as a child, it continues to grow today. My journey through life, however, has proven one thing for sure—in addition to faith, my obedience to God's commandments is also necessary.

Yet despite my lack of obedience to God's commandments over the course of my life, He still honored my faith throughout high school, college, and my professional football career. As a child, I'd always tell my brothers and mother, "When I grow up, I'm going to go to the University of Michigan, become a lawyer, and play professional basketball! Then I'm gonna buy Mom a house and take a trip around the entire world!" And thanks to God using Mr. Pipkin, my sixth grade homeroom teacher, I received some tough love and also learned how to dream big! Every year Mr. Pipkin would have each of his students complete a "Scrapbook of Destiny." In this scrapbook, we had to illustrate what our future would be like—education, career, house, and family—any and every detail was to be accounted for! I remember cutting out images of a beautiful family, a big house, and a college degree, in addition to many other things.

As a result of my faith that God would allow me to accomplish and obtain all I had included in my scrapbook of destiny—I can now honestly say, I did it, including buying my mom her very first home after she had been a renter her whole life! (Actually, I have yet to get my law degree, but I'm still planning on it one day! And of course, I never made it to the NBA—but those guys are soft anyway...just kidding!)

Due to my faith, God prospered me and gave me all the desires of my heart, yet I lived a foolish and frivolous lifestyle! I did what I wanted to do—wasting time, energy, and millions of dollars in the process—until my lifestyle began to change. Following my surrender to Christ, I remember hearing God say, "In order to get you to increase your level of obedience, I needed to take away all I had given you because of your faith."

Upon hearing this, after walking away from the NFL and blowing over half of what I earned, I felt compelled to change my lifestyle. I began selling homes, luxury cars, and cashing in a number of other investments. Wearing twenty, thirty, and forty thousand dollar watches while encouraging groups of young people to pursue purpose rather than possessions seemed totally hypocritical. So I even sold my prized collection of luxury watches. As all of the fame and status that came with playing professional football began to fade away, so did all of the women I had grown accustomed to wasting time with. To my surprise, I felt relieved—and a seed of meekness was planted within me.

You see, while growing up I experienced what it felt like to be extremely poor and on welfare. I became accustomed to the five of us living in roach-infested apartments—occasionally having eviction notices taped to our front door. Yet on the other hand, my years in the NFL allowed me the opportunity to experience an affluent lifestyle! I could walk into any store and purchase whatever I wanted, own million dollar homes, have sex with beautiful women all around the world, and literally party like a rock star.

As a result of all of my combined life experiences—good and bad, negative and positive—I have arrived at this single truth: I do not want to be poor, nor do I want to be the wealthiest man in the world. *All I want now is Jesus Christ!* As Jesus said in the eighth chapter of Mark, verse thirty-six,

> *For what shall it profit a man, if he shall gain the whole world, and lose his own soul?*

I spent most of my life attempting to gain the world and all of its pleasures, but I was losing my soul in the process. Now, however, I'm determined to spend the rest of my days on this earth pursuing and teaching others about the man who, over the course of my entire life, has become my best friend, my counselor, my protector, my savior, my provider, my healer—Jesus Christ!

As a result of the decision I made to change my lifestyle and pursue Christ, I have had to part ways with people for a variety of reasons. With some, we are simply headed in different directions. With others, they profess and believe that Jesus Christ is not the Son of God. And some just don't understand me and why I live my life the way I do now.

"There are going to be people from your past who will attempt to come back into your life," God said to me one day, "and when they do, I want you to ask them this question—'Are you going to heaven?' And after they reply, I want you to say to them, 'Okay, I'll see you there. Take care.' By telling people this, you are expressing a hope to see them in heaven. You are also letting them know, however, that I don't want you to travel the same path while you are here on this earth." The Bible poses a similar question in the Old Testament:

Can two walk together, except they be agreed? (Amos 3:3).

The answer to this question is clearly no. Which is why, although I choose to love everyone, I have separated myself from certain individuals from my past.

These days, I spend most of my time using the many gifts God gave me, of which music happens to be one. Over the years, I have always enjoyed singing and playing musical instruments. There was even a night during my freshman year at the University of Michigan that I was forced to sing in front of the entire team at dinner. My nerves were a mess, but I sang my heart out. I did such a good job, in fact, that a few of my teammates shouted, "Yeah buddy, you'll be singing every night!"

That didn't happen, but I remember singing quite often then and over the next few years—during dinner or at events on campus. There were even times my teammates and I would attend open mic events and talent shows. While seated in the crowd, it never failed—just as the master of ceremonies asked the judges to begin tallying the votes, my teammates would begin shouting from the back of the room, "NOOOO! NOOOO! WAIT, WE GOT ONE MO SINGER!" as they tried to persuade me to go up and sing.

During one of the few occasions I got up to sing, the MC looked at me and said, "You want him to do what?! He's got too many muscles to be trying to sing!" After letting out a half laugh along with the rest of the crowd, I grabbed the microphone, shutting him and all of the other doubters up.

Along with singing, I have always loved playing musical instruments. The first instrument I ever learned to play was the trumpet in fifth grade. I wanted to play it because my dad blew the horn.

Over the years, I also taught myself how to play the piano. In fact, while seated in a lecture at the University of Michigan one day, I noticed a beautiful brown upright at the front of the large room. And from that day forward, on several different occasions, I would make the almost two-mile trek back up to campus in the evenings, my trumpet case in hand, to perform in my "concert hall." After making sure no one was around, I would imagine a crowd of people seated in the enormous auditorium and play my trumpet. Then, after finishing my solo, I would let my fingers dance on the piano.

In January 2010, I took a few guitar lessons, and then taught myself from there. Now, whenever I find myself getting a little unsettled or unnerved by people or circumstances, I simply pick up my guitar or take a seat at my piano and let the music flow! I especially love the guitar because I can take it with me everywhere I go.

Actually, when I was in South Africa, just before getting into bed one night, one of the young boys pointed to my guitar case. "What is this?" he asked.

"It's a guitar," I replied.

"Wow! Will you play a song for us, pleeease?"

After making a deal with the boys, which entailed them singing a song first, I began playing the song I wrote to put my daughter to sleep at night. Within five minutes, all five of the boys were fast asleep! What a beautiful moment.

Today, God is teaching me the value of the gifts and talents He has placed inside of me. After wasting millions of dollars and the small measure of influence that came with

Plant Water Grow

celebrity status, God reminded me, "Everything I want you to use to do my work I placed inside of you before the day you were conceived. From the music that pours out of you, to the well of emotions you have drawn from to write this book, and even the seed you planted to create your daughter—I placed it all inside of you."

I sat in total amazement after hearing God's words. I thought of His many gifts to me. *All of the time I wasted—the years I spent chasing my selfish desires and all the world had to offer—while all along the Lord wanted me to use the gifts He placed inside of me.*

And I have been given many gifts—my athletic ability, my musical talent, and my ability to write. But despite all of my many gifts, I am most thankful for God making me grow.

IMMUNITY

On February 23, 2011, I arose from my bed shortly after midnight and began to type my life's story, marking the start of what would be a four-day period of extensive writing. My writing was merely an act of obedience—a response to a prompting by the Holy Spirit. At first, I thought the purpose for writing this book was to simply share an assortment of personal experiences from the first thirty-three years of my life. God's purpose for me writing about my life, however, turned out to be quite different.

Looking back at my journey through life has brought a great deal of perspective. Little did I know that God would use my choices—and the consequences of those choices—to produce an "immunity" to the *love of the world*. Which, ultimately, led to my choosing to embrace God's unwavering love for me.

Let me explain: as a child I needed to receive the chicken pox vaccination—a live-virus vaccine and a much weaker strain of the chicken pox—so that my body would become immune to, or resist, the illness later in life. Similarly, God allowed me to ingest a seed of "the world's love", in order for my spirit to, eventually, become immune to it. Yet, unlike the six-week period it took for my body to become immune to the chicken pox, becoming immune to the "world's love" took every bit of thirty-three years.

You see, after the world measured and calculated my ability to run, jump, and endure and inflict physical punishment, I became an asset to the world—all at the ripe age of thirteen. Thereafter, the world placed me on "All Star Teams," offered me a chance to earn a college education, and, ultimately, the opportunity to earn a decent living in exchange for my physical ability.

Unfortunately, I chose to ignore my careless nature when it came to money, not to mention my weakness and susceptibility to beautiful women, and fully embraced the world's love. In doing so, I received fame, fortune, and all of the many pleasures that came with the life of a professional athlete. The love of the world was tangible—I could see it, taste it, smell it, feel it. Regardless of how the "world's love" manifested in my life—a beautiful woman laying next to me in bed, seven figure checks I deposited into my bank account, my luxurious possessions, or my growing stardom—there reached a point in my life that I could no longer imagine my life without it. I became lost in a sea of my own sin.

Then came the truth.

The truth is, the *dysfunctional* love the world offers, despite its mesmerizing and alluring affect, seeks to flatter, not encourage; it's selfish, not giving; it's cold and distant, not warm and comforting; it's conditional, and extremely unreliable. All this kind of love can produce is selfishness, greed, hatred, and Godlessness. I suffered at the hands of the world's love, because it never delivered what it promised. Ironically, each time I suffered at the hands of the world's love, I ran to God for comfort and support. That is, until the day God revealed to me His *true nature*.

You see, I had thought of God most of my life as being "reactive," meaning that I immediately would run to Him to save myself from hurt or harm. But the Lord told me one day, "Be careful when you ask me to react to the negative circumstances and consequences in your life, which result from your deliberate disobedience to my instructions, because *when I 'react' it is never favorable to men!* Think of the cities of Sodom and Ghomorah, or Noah and the ark—these are instances in which I reacted. In both instances I destroyed both the evil and the sin, as well as the lives of those who would not obey my instructions!"

Hearing God's words, I instantly became convicted. *Lord, forgive me for asking you to react to the negative circumstances and consequences in my life that have come as a result of my disobedience.*

Following my prayer, I wrote down more of the understanding God gave me:

The truth is this: God's true nature is "proactive"—meaning God always warns us of our sin, making us aware of our disobedience and wrongdoing because He doesn't want us to suffer the consequences that result from our disobedience to His instructions. God warns us by sending messages and signs through other individuals, negative circumstances, dreams, nightmares, as well as through reading the Bible.

There are many proactive measures God took in His attempts to prevent me from suffering. In the end, I chose to ignore these warnings. But now, by His grace, I have learned to thank God and acknowledge His proactive activity in my life, which has prevented me from suffering pain like I have in the past.

As a result of my unwillingness to heed God's promptings, I suffered persecution and judgment—both privately and publicly. Answering a phone call from my oldest brother Jason one day, he asked in a tone filled with concern, "Hey, this guy I know said something about women writing all kinds of crazy things about you on some website. What's up with that?"

I said, "Man, although most of it's false, I hate to say that some of that stuff is true. I have done a lot of dirt, man, and hurt a lot of women. So I'm not mad at them for talking bad about me. Jesus was persecuted and He *wasn't* guilty of any sin. So with all the sins I *have* committed, how could I dare get mad at them for bad-mouthing me? I can't. Don't worry about it man, I can handle it."

Did reading and hearing about some of the negative things women had to say about me sting a little? Sure, I'm human. But nothing hurts worse than knowing that I deserved to suffer persecution for the way I carelessly lived my life. At the end of the day, the negative comments and remarks I read made me even more determined to be like Christ. I guess God does have a way of taking our failures and using them to make us more like Jesus—I should know, I'm living proof.

Finally, after years of suffering emotionally, physically, and most importantly, spiritually, I chose to stop using my body to entertain the world. And so I became useless to it, no longer profitable or entertaining. I watched as the "world's love" for me quickly turned into persecution, resentment, disdain and hatred. In the blink of an eye, the world's celebration of me changed to criticism and condemnation.

"He was never really that good of a player anyway, so I say good riddance."

"He wasn't a team player."

"He was overpaid anyway."

"He sucked!"

The list goes on.

Little did I know, the world was destined to hate me, because the truth of the matter is that the world—despite it's efforts, and me wanting to be chosen by it—couldn't choose me, because I had already been chosen, as Jesus stated:

> *If the world hate you, ye know that it hated me before it hated you. If ye were of the world, the world would love his own: but because ye are not of the world, but I have chosen you out of the world, therefore the world hateth you. (John 15:18-19)*

Despite being hated, there was one thing I was still useful for: gossip and negative headlines. Once rumors began to circulate on the Internet about my sexual indiscretions, as well as the news of me being cited for child abuse, the world once again found me entertaining and profitable.

Even though my athletic talent was enough cause for the world to offer me its love, before I was conceived in my mother's womb, *God knew me and loved me for simply being me* (Jeremiah 1:5). In fact, out of His love for me, God allowed the world to love me conditionally. He knew that despite my *hefty* appetite for the world's love and all it offered, one day I would develop a bad taste for it—ultimately rejecting it and becoming immune to the sin it produces all together.

Now God didn't look at me one day and say, "Because Ian is intelligent, strong, can run really fast, and hit really hard, I'm going to give him my love." He instead gave me His love without any conditions. In addition to His love, He also gave me free will—the freedom to make my own decisions. Sadly,

Plant Water Grow

with this freedom I wrongfully embraced the world's *conditional* love for me, rather than God's *unconditional* love for me.

Throughout my entire life, the love I sought from the cheering crowds, countless women, close friends, and even my own family members has failed me. In fact, there were even times my own mother's love failed me. During my junior year in high school, my mother—out of her own desire for love—allowed a man who was not her husband to move into our apartment. After my brothers and I failed to change her mind, I decided to move in with my aunt for a year. For the first time ever, I went weeks without speaking to my mother. I felt as if she was choosing to love her boyfriend over me. *How could she let this guy come between us?* I wondered. All the years she preached and taught my brothers and me about living a holy and righteous life appeared to go down the drain. She became a hypocrite. After realizing that he was simply using her, she kicked him out and the strain on our relationship eased.

Did my mother love me? Certainly. In fact, to this day my mother's love for me exceeds that of any other person I know—but even her love does not compare to the love God has always had, and still has, for me. Since realizing this truth, the seed of God's love within me has fully bloomed.

God so *loved* me that He sent His only begotten Son, Jesus Christ, to save me (John 3:16).

The loneliness, rejection, heartache, and pain I suffered, as I desperately searched for unconditional love from others, will never compare to how I felt the moment my heart broke for Christ.

While writing one afternoon, I heard God say, "The fear and heartache you felt when I told you that you were useless to me was because you feared losing my love. Over the course of your life you have searched for unconditional love in many places—family members, women, friends, cheering crowds—and as a result, your heart has been broken and damaged. But all of the heartache and pain you have experienced from the failing love of others will never come close to what you experienced on the day your heart broke for me. For the first time ever, I showed you a glimpse of *my* broken heart—broken over all of the pain your sinful actions caused—and your heart finally became broken for *me*. Up until that point in your life, I had been your only source of *unconditional* love and, for the first time in your life, you feared losing me more than anyone or anything else."

In Romans 8:38-39, the Scriptures remind us that nothing can separate us from the love of God. Regardless of having known this fact, the thought of disappointing God had made me wonder if God was going to take His love away from me because of all of my sexually immoral behavior, idolatry, and unbelief. I felt condemned.

But I was wrong.

As I read Paul's words in Romans 8:1:

> *There is therefore now no condemnation to them which are in Christ Jesus, who walk not after the flesh, but after the spirit.*

Romans 8:34 takes this one-step further. It reminds us that Jesus is at the right hand of the Father interceding for us. While I was busy pursuing the desires of my own lust, Christ was busy petitioning the Father to pour out His mercy and grace upon me—and for that I am grateful. My heart was broken for Christ after realizing the pain and suffering my sin caused Him. Now, being *immune* to the "world's love" and with a clear heart, mind, body, and soul—as well as a heart broken for Christ—I reject the love of the world and embrace God's *unrelenting, undying, unfailing* and *everlasting love*.

In Paul's last words to Timothy, the self-proclaimed chief of sinners states:

> *As for me, my life has already been poured out as an offering to God. The time of my death is near. I have fought the good fight, I have finished the race, and I have remained faithful. And now the prize awaits me—the crown of righteousness, that the Lord, the righteous Judge, will give me on the day of his return. And the prize is not just for me but for all who eagerly look forward to his glorious return" (1 Timothy 4:6-8, nlt).*

As I begin to think about my own death, a sense of urgency and desperation envelops my heart when I think of all the people who have never heard the gospel of Jesus Christ. In May of 2011, while quietly reciting first Corinthians chapter three and verse six to myself as I sat on my living room floor, three words came to mind—*Plant, Water, Grow*. More than simply the title of a book and online journal—*plant, water, grow* is the Lord's directive to me. Now, more than ever, Christ desires me to: *plant* seeds of the gospel, *water* people with God's Word, so that He can make them *grow*.

God once said, "Ian, there is no need for you to exercise patience if you have nothing to look forward to." Therefore, as I journey onward and *God continues to make me grow*, I look forward to Him completely uprooting every bad seed that has been planted inside me over the past three decades—the world's dysfunctional love, violence, anger, hatred, bitterness, loneliness, rejection, arrogance, promiscuity, deception and lust—so that roots from good seeds: humility, compassion, goodness, peace, joy, faithfulness, gentleness, meekness, longsuffering, self-control and God's *unconditional* love, can dig deeper and deeper inside me.

Before surrendering my life to Christ, what I feared most was the thought of having to sacrifice my relationships with women, my material possessions, and even my professional football career for the sake of Christ. I had become accustomed to and dependent upon the physical comfort and false sense of security I received from women, my job, and my possessions. Today, however, is a different story—as I am comforted by the Holy Spirit, the Word of God, the encouraging words of my spiritual forefathers, and the brothers and sisters in Christ with whom I walk today.

Before Christ entered the world, God created the ritual of sacrifice as a way to provide an opportunity for His people to make atonement for their disobedience to His laws and commandments. When Christ entered the world and died on the cross, His death became the last sacrifice God would require to atone for the sin of the entire world.

Today, all Christ desires from those of us who believe in Him is our willingness. Two of my favorite accounts in the Bible, both in the New Testament, display both this willingness and unwillingness: the account of the woman who gave her last two coins in the offering and the account of the young rich ruler. I used to marvel, thinking the woman sacrificed all the money she had. The truth, however, is that she did not really sacrifice anything—she was simply *willing* to give all she had. On the other hand, when Christ asked the young rich ruler if he was willing to sell all that he had and give to the poor in exchange for riches in heaven, the young ruler was *unwilling*.

In reading about my life up to this point, you're probably wondering, "So what's next?" Well, although I cannot provide you with a complete, detailed answer, I can say one thing. In the Old Testament, Isaiah says,

Also I heard the voice of the Lord, saying, Whom Shall I send, and who will go for us? Then said I, Here am I, send me (Isaiah 6:8).

On September 7, 2011, I sold my home and many of my possessions. I felt God was sending me on a new journey—to "go" proclaim and teach to the gospel of Jesus Christ. Presently, I am living in a 25-foot long trailer just outside of Los Angeles, California. Lord willing, I will travel from city-to-city, state-to-state, and country-to-country, with my bag full of seeds and, *the living water*, Jesus Christ.

Throughout this entire project, God's directive to me has been to be completely transparent about my life. And although it has grieved me at times to read about my former self—in addition to using me to plant and water seeds of the gospel in others—I am beyond humbled and honored that God has chosen a sinner like me to serve as an example of the supernatural transformation that occurs when someone is, *receptive of His seeds, receptive of His water, and He makes them grow.*

My great hope is that my life has—in some small way—illustrated the height, the depth, and the width of God's love. Amen.

Travel along with me as God continues to make me grow…

www.plantwatergrow.com

CPSIA information can be obtained at www.ICGtesting.com
Printed in the USA
LVOW111417090412

276811LV00002B/1/P